COKER'S JAZZ KEYBOARD

For Pianists and Non-Pianists
(class or individual study)

TABLE OF CONTENTS

PREFACE

The piano is a magnificent instrument, extending far beyond its use by virtuoso performers. It is such a standard in our musical environment. Young people are often introduced to music via the piano, even though both child and parent may view such study as a precedent to the selection of some other, more intensely studied, instrument at a later time. Sometimes the individual will indeed select piano as his/her ultimate instrument, but even if some other instrument is eventually chosen, the piano is likely to remain at least a companion or secondary instrument. A musician's home seems incomplete without a piano, even if no one in the house is a pianist by trade. Piano is the most common instrument for accompaniment in classical music, and in jazz it is a rare novelty to find a group that is not using a piano. A pianist is likely to find work when players of all other instruments cannot, as it is an instrument capable of independence from all other instruments, producing melody, chords, and rhythm. In the right hands, the piano can sound like a large ensemble. It is this multi-functional capacity that places piano (and, of course, other keyboard instruments, such as organ, harpsichord, vibraphones, etc.) in a unique class... it is capable of independent functioning, carrying all essential musical elements. Another enormously popular instrument, the guitar, shares this capacity, but the piano is unrivalled as an instrument which affords visual understanding as well. That is, the guitar fretboard is too uniform in appearance to permit the same sort of quick, easy visual understanding that is possible on the unique white and black key arrangement found on the piano. Consequently it is the piano that has become a sort of musical computer board for players of all instruments.

A piano is also much like a typewriter; that is, used by non-pianists as well as pianists, as the typewriter is used by both non-typists and typists. A 'hunt-and-peck' typist may not be able to type 90 words per minute, but goals and results are obtained, nonetheless. Likewise, the piano may be used by non-pianists to obtain goals and results that are difficult or impossible to obtain on instruments like saxophone, trumpet, bass, trombone, drums, flute, etc. There are a number of reasons for a non-pianist to study Jazz Keyboard. Among them are:

(1) as an aid in studying and hearing various chord structures;

(2) as an aid in studying and hearing various scales with chords;

(3) as a means of learning chord progressions to tunes;

(4) as a means to audition tunes in fake books (songbooks) which have never been heard by the reader;

(5) to accompany self as a singer;

(6) to accompany self as an instrumentalist, by taping a keyboard accompaniment of a chord, progression, tune, etc.;

(7) to accompany a student or friend;

(8) to fill in for a pianist at a rehearsal or performance, should the pianist not be there for any reason;

(9) to coach an inexperienced pianist in an ensemble;

(10) as an aid in composing and arranging;

(11) as an aid in teaching improvisation, theory, composition, arranging, etc.;

(12) to use as a secondary instrument in the professional field.

The pianist has more obvious reasons to study Jazz Keyboard. Piano is his/her chosen instrument, and yet instruction in the jazz style is not as easy to locate as one might imagine. Colleges and universities are very often lacking in instructors of piano who are even attuned to jazz, much less willing or able to teach same effectively (my apologies to the capable, hard-working few). Considering the popularity of piano and the need, in particular, for jazz instruction, it is surprising that there are so few good methods available. Perhaps the great demand for performing pianists is so great that few of them have the time to teach, devise methods, and write books. Jazz Keyboard has evolved from fifteen years of teaching jazz piano classes at various universities. That the system works is a foregone conclusion. Although it was chiefly designed to serve the non-pianist, my classes are frequently taken by pianists, who tell me that they needed it, benefited from it, and couldn't have learned it from their piano instructor. The beneficial results and their practical application come very quickly, and my former students, even those of fifteen years ago, tell me that it was the most important course in the jazz curriculum. They may have been primarily interested in improvisation or arranging classes, but the jazz piano course seemed to give them something that could be utilized quickly and fed directly into their study of, say, improvisation or arranging. I must say that I have enjoyed hearing a dozen or so students who move from learning where Middle C is located to reading the chord progression to a tune at the end of the second hourly meeting.

Jazz Keyboard is divided into three sections, each section requiring approximately one term (semester or quarter) to complete, as a class method, depending upon the length and frequency of the classes and the general level of ability and effort. An individual, especially a pianist, could complete a section in considerably less time, probably.

JERRY COKER
Big Creek Music Seminary
Route 3, Box 225
Marshall, North Carolina 28753

INTRODUCTION

The first and most important task for the jazz pianist is to produce chords. Jazz is a harmonically-based music. Melodies are important, but they are often played by another member of a group, especially wind instruments. Improvisation is important, but all players in a group are expected to improvise, and when the pianist is not improvising, he/she is still chording (comping) for everyone else. Furthermore, chords must be learned in order to learn the proper scales for each, which form the foundation for improvising. This book will not emphasize the art of improvisation, as such a study is lengthy and has been covered very well in already-existing books, to which the reader will be directed later in the book. Rhythm is important, too, but it is best learned by imitation and transcriptions (suggestions will be made later in the book for learning good comping rhythms, though very few will appear in this method in a specific form).

The chord progressions of tunes used in jazz are nearly always given in chord symbols, which the keyboard player is expected to decipher and arrange into an attractive chord voicing. As a new symbol will appear about every two to eight beats, on the average, the pianist has to develop quick responses in order to find and play each chord within its assigned duration. The chord symbol does not prescribe the voicing, and yet there are a vast number of voicing possibilities (voicing a chord in a 1-3-5-7 order, in close position, is not really acceptable). A glance at Dan Haerle's Jazz/Rock Voicings For The Contemporary Keyboard Player 1. will reveal the awesome number of possibilities. Chord voicings have a number of variable elements:

(1) the number of chord tones to be included;
(2) the number of chord tones to be doubled, if any;
(3) the order in which the chord tones are stacked;
(4) the spacing (distances between chord tones in the voicing);
(5) whether the chord can be extended, added to, or altered;
(6) deciding what chord tone will be on the top of the voicing; and
(7) deciding whether the bottom note shall be the root or something else.

Obviously that would be a lot to think about... too much, in fact, as by the time a pianist has pondered all that, the chord's duration is long gone. The answer lies in not pondering all the possibilities, at least not at the start of study, and not when reading a progression for the first time. The student should learn one effective voicing at a time, until it is mastered, or until it can be produced quickly enough to keep up with the rapidly passing symbols. Then other voicing variables may be introduced, one by one. Some of the best comping pianists use a surprisingly small number of chord voicings. It is not the number of different voicings which make them effective players, but their ability to use a small number of choice voicings in an effective way.

In using formulized voicings, it should be pointed out that the hands will frequently be ahead of the brain. Since we are trying to quicken our response to the sight of a chord symbol by using a prescribed, formula voicing, we are momentarily bypassing the brain in its ponderous choices. We need not be bothered by such automatic responses, for the present anyway, as the voicings are known to be effective from the start, and we will have plenty of retrospective time in which to allow the brain to catch up to the hands, thanks to the frequent need to play the same progression ad infinitum in rehearsals and performances.

1. Studio P/R, Hialeah, FL

Always learn each new voicing in <u>all</u> keys, as jazz tunes and standards tend to modulate frequently. "Cherokee", for example, is in the reasonable key of B-flat, but the bridge (B section) passes through the keys of B, A, and G. If you are a saxophone player or a trumpet player, you also want to remember that concert-pitched instruments (i.e., piano, bass, trombone, and flute) frequently play in E-flat, A-flat, and D-flat.

Don't lean on the sustaining pedal, especially in medium to fast tempos, as it tends to destroy pulse-feeling. A ballad is about the only time you might need the sustaining pedal, and it can be overused there, too. Especially be careful not to sustain when moving to a new chord.

Select your fingering of chords carefully, using simple logic, then try to be consistent about such fingerings. For example, if you have to reach a wide interval, like a seventh, don't try to use adjacent fingers, or even something like your little finger and your middle finger. Likewise, don't finger small intervals, like thirds, with the thumb and little finger.

Don't get in the habit of playing chords in a broken fashion (playing one note after another, instead of all notes together) or arpeggiating chords repeatedly, like the classical Alberti Bass (a la Mozart). Inexperienced pianists usually form such habits either because they feel self-concious about the spaces of time between chords, or because they have primarily played without a bassist or drummer (as a <u>single</u> performer, perhaps in a restaurant).

If the reader is a teacher, and planning to use this method as a class method for jazz piano, the Appendix contains suggestions to help you have a smoothly operating course. You may want to supplement this book with more tunes for reading, perhaps from a fakebook, a songbook, or something like Jamey Aebersold's <u>New Approach To Improvisation</u>, Vols. 22, 23, and 25, which contain forty-two standard tunes, each in three keys. The booklets may be purchased without the play-along record, if you choose, <u>or</u> you might want to have the record as well, so your students can play with the recorded bass and drum tracks (the records are in stereo, with bass and drums on one side and piano and drums on the other). You might also want to use the record as a good illustration of piano comping. The series (28 volumes at this printing) are extremely helpful and others will be recommended from this series as the method progresses.

SECTION 1

It will often be necessary to refer to a particular octave or register of the piano. Rather than to learn the formal names of **each** octave (Contra, Great, Small, etc.), it will suffice, for our purposes, to simply learn the location of Middle C. Since, however, electric pianos often have fewer than the conventional 88 keys found on the acoustic piano, the figures given below become necessary. If the reader studies class piano in a school-owned electric keyboard room, the chances are very good that the units being used there are the Wurlitzer keyboards shown in Figure 2.

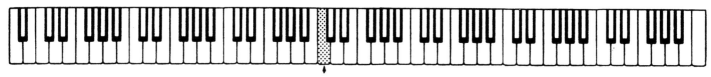

MIDDLE C

FIGURE 1
The 88-key Acoustic Piano

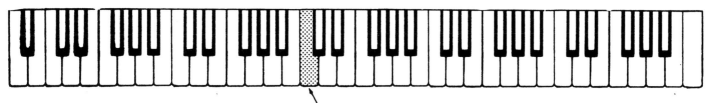

MIDDLE C

FIGURE 2
The 64-key Wurlitzer Piano
(electric)

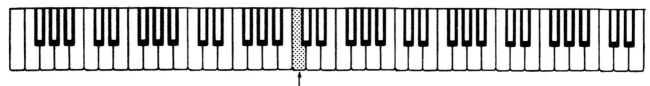

MIDDLE C

FIGURE 3
The 73-key Fender Rhodes Piano
(electric)

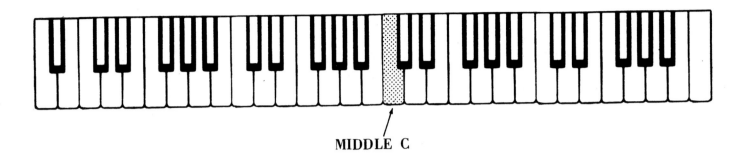

MIDDLE C

FIGURE 4
The 49-key Yamaha Piano
(electric)

For the reader who is totally unfamiliar with the piano keyboard, Figure 5 shows how to find any note within one octave (C to C). Note, in Figure 1 (The 88-key acoustic piano), how the pattern of two black keys - space - three black keys - space repeats itself all the way up the keyboard, though the pattern is fragmented at the bottom because the lowest note is A instead of C. This symmetry is what makes the piano easy to understand, visually.

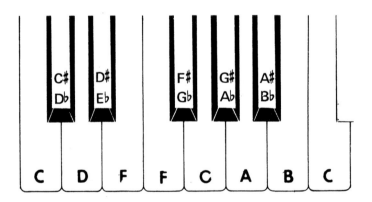

FIGURE 5

For the reader who knows the names of the notes on the keyboard, but is unfamiliar with the relationship between the notes on the keyboard and the **written** (notated) form of those notes, **Figure 6** should make that clear.

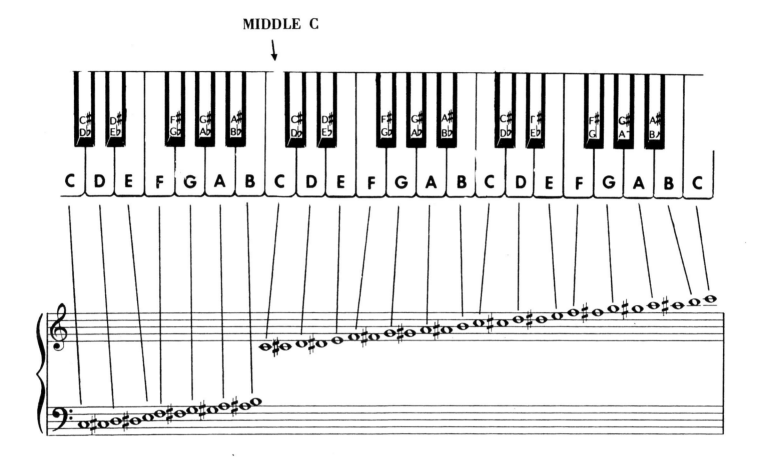

FIGURE 6

The 1-7-3-5 Voicing

There are two basic types of chord voicings, those which use the root of the chord at the bottom of the voicing, and those which do not. The latter type will be taken up toward the end of Section 1 and continued through Section 2. It is easier to begin with voicings which have chord roots at the bottom, as the player can achieve a better orientation to chord structure, chord function, even chord identity, as there may be times, at the outset, when the hands will get ahead of the eyes and the brain to the point that the player can become lost in the progression. Being able to glance at the lowest note being played and know that it represents the root of the chord can be a help at such times.

Although, as stated earlier, there are many ways to voice a chord, restricting ourselves to **a root voicing** narrows the number of possibilities. Then if we further restrict ourselves to voicings which omit **doublings** (chord tones that are duplicated in another octave of the same chord voicing), we reduce the possibilities even further. We will, for now at least, also avoid voicings that are so widely-spaced that we cannot attack all notes simultaneously (the average hand can only reach about an octave plus one step). For the moment, we won't be adding chord extensions above the seventh (i.e., ninths, elevenths, thirteenths) or altered chord notes, which reduce the possibilities even further. Finally, we won't use voicings which have irregular, unattractive spacings (good spacing usually means having wider intervals near the bottom of the voicing and smaller intervals near the top — if we reverse this tendency, the results are usually unsatisfactory). With all this in mind, only about two possibilities survive; the 1-7-3-5- and the 1-5-7-3 voicings (see Figure 7). This text will concentrate on the former, thought he student may wish to work with both. The digits used to describe the voicing (i.e., 1-7-3-5-) are pulled from the scale implied by the chord. So, for example, if we are playing a **C major chord**, we think of a C major scale (C,D,E, F,G,A,B, C), assign respective digits to each note (C is 1, D is 2, E is 3, etc.), then extract the ones needed for the 1-7-3-5 voicing (C,B,E, and G).

FIGURE 7

Figure 8 shows how the notated 1-7-3-5 voicing of Figure 7 appears on the keyboard. Note the position of Middle C, so that the student will know which register of the keyboard is being used. Also note that the lowest two notes of the voicing are played with the left hand and the other two notes are played with the right. Numbering the fingers of the hands from 1 to 5, with the thumbs being 1 and the little finger being 5, the fingerings of the voicing are suggested at the bottom of Figure 8.

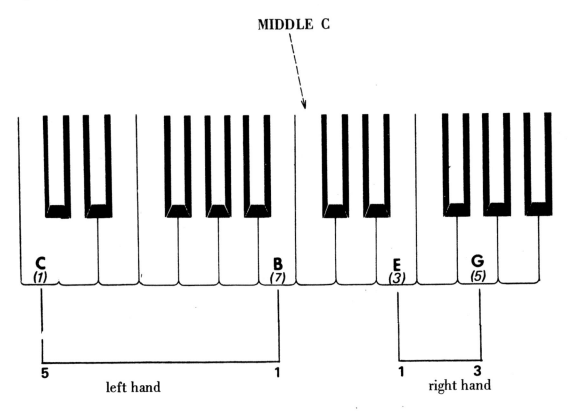

FIGURE 8

Now play Exercise 1 (below), using the same fingerings as shown in Figure 8. Since the exercise is in the key of C (indicated by the symbol "C:"), there are no sharps or flats to be played (in other words, no black keys), therefore once the student has placed his/her hands on the correct keys for the first chord (see Figure 8), the hands simply move up one key at a time, staying on the white keys. Be careful not to expand or contract either hand, or alter the distance between the hands, while progressing up the keyboard. After moving up, step-by-step, to where the hands are playing the same notes as the starting place, but an octave higher, repeat that chord and begin descending by step until reaching the original starting place. The student who can read music will find it easy to play Exercise 1 without needing to use the foregoing 'crutches'.

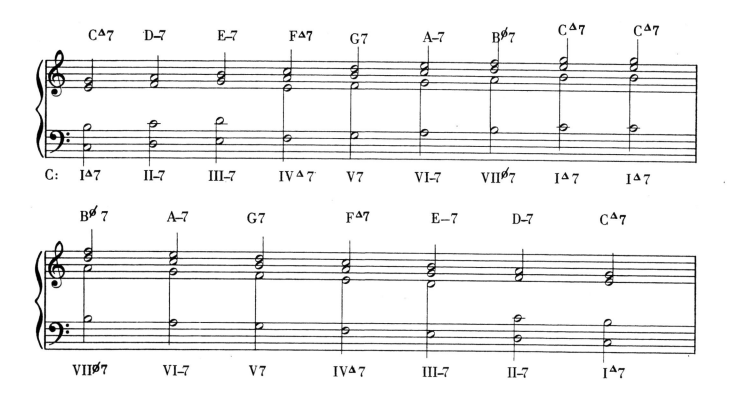

EXERCISE 1

Exercise 1 should present little or no problem to the reader, in that it is very easy, physically, to perform. And yet the training is well under way, already. The voicing is pleasant enough, the hands are beginning to be familiar with the keyboard, and the mind and the ears have been introduced to a diatonic (scalar) system of chords contained within every key that includes four different kinds of chords! Note that above the exercise are lettered symbols (C, D, E, etc.) and below the exercise are numbered (Roman numerals) symbols following the key-declaring symbol, "C:". The common lead sheet to a song usually comprises the notated melody and lettered symbols, rather than Roman numerals. However, it is helpful to at least think of the Roman numerals sometimes, as they indicate the functions of the chords in relation to the key-note, make the progression easier to memorize, and easier to play in another key. They also show what is common between two different keys (by placing them into a sort of universality), and that's the main reason they have been included at this point. Looking ahead, for the moment, to Exercise 2, in which the voicings of Exercise 1 have been transposed to the key of E-flat, note that the chord symbols for the Roman numerals are identical; that is, the "I" chords of both keys are the same, as are the II chords, the III chords, and so on. The meaning of the symbols have not yet been explained, however.

Along with either the lettered or Roman numeral symbols, there are other aspects of the symbol, such as triangles, dashes, circles with vertical lines running through them, and Arabic numerals. These signify the exact structural properties of the chords (as well as their sound and function). Looking at a keyboard or any of the preceding figures of a keyboard, it will be noticed that there are two places within each octave where there is a space between black notes; that is, places within each octave where black keys have been 'omitted'. In fact this is precisely why the keyboard is so easy to understand and use for computing distances (intervals) between notes, much as we use a ruler or a measuring cup with gradations. But those spaces where there are no black keys are telling us something else, as well, namely that a C major scale (or any other key, for that matter) is **not** a symmetrical scale. Between E and F, and between B and C, where there is no black note, the interval between them is smaller (called a half-step or a minor second interval) than between all the white notes which **do** have a black key between them (where the interval is called a whole-step or a major second interval). This lack of symmetry is what makes it necessary to add sharps and flats (black notes, usually) when trying to produce a major scale in any other key than C. But that same lack of symmetry also causes the chord-types (indicated by the triangles, dashes, etc.) to vary as the hands move up the scale-chords, because the intervals between the root (1) and 7, or between 7 and 3, or 3 and 5, for example are different, even though we are staying in one key (the key of C, in Exercise 1). Looking at the keyboard, compare the distance between the bottom two notes (1 and 7) of the C (or I) chord and the distance between the 1 and 7 of the D (II) chord. Note that in the C chord the 7 (B) is only a half-step away from the octave (C), because there is no black note between B and C, whereas in the D chord the distance between 1 (D) and 7 (C) is slightly smaller, because there is a black key between C and the octave above the chord root (D). The interval between 3 and 5 of the two chords are also different, again because of the different number of half-steps and/or black notes between their respective 3's and 5's.

Figure 9 shows the names for the chord symbols used thus far, along with alternate symbols. Chord symbols are not completely standardized, therefore one must be prepared to interpret more than one symbol for the same chord-type.

SYMBOL	NAME	ALTERNATE SYMBOLS
△7	major seventh chord	M7 Maj.7 or letter by itself
-7	minor seventh chord	m7 min.7 or dash(−) by itself
7	dominant seventh chord, (or simply) seventh chord	(none)
∅7	half-diminished seventh chord, or minor seventh chord with a flatted fifth	m7($\flat$5) m7(−5)

FIGURE 9

Looking again at Exercise 1, note that Roman numeral I and IV are both major seventh chords, II, III, and VI are minor seventh chords, V is a dominant seventh chord, and VII is a half-diminished seventh chord. Exercise 2 (in E-flat major) will show the same pattern of chord structures, as will all other major keys. Once the student has learned the sound of each chord-type and has learned to observe which Roman numeral chord is being played in any major key, the ear will begin to help the player to determine whether or not the chord is being played correctly. Bear in mind, when reading the progressions to various tunes, however, that chords within a key are sometimes altered to become a different type than the one normally found within a given key. In particular, II and VI are frequently altered from their usual quality of a minor seventh chord by raising the 3rd of the chord, causing it to become a dominant seventh chord (the type usually only found on V). These are called **secondary dominants** and commonplace from Bach to the present.

In preparation for playing Exercise 2, which is in E-flat major, review the procedure used for arriving at an understanding of the exercise in C major. First the E-flat major scale must be constructed, as it will tell us which notes must be altered in order to retain the scale structure of C major, which was built of whole-steps, except between 3 and 4, and between 7 and 8(1).

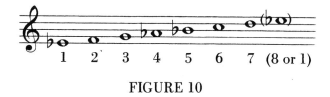

FIGURE 10

It can be seen that in order to retain the major scale structure, with its particular order of whole-steps and half-steps, it is necessary to add flats to three notes of the scale: B, E, and A. These flatted notes will have to be remembered throughout the playing of Exercise 2 (unless, of course, the player is merely reading), as every chord of the scale has at least one of those flatted notes in it, as one or more members of the chord. To be sure that Exercise 2 is started correctly, find the notes of the I chord (E-flat) first, by looking at Figure 11.

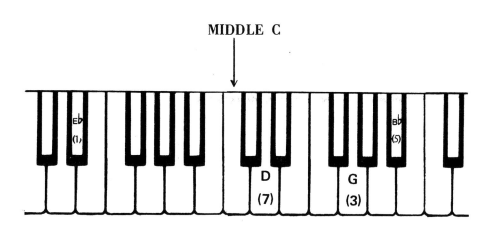

FIGURE 11

Now play Exercise 2.

EXERCISE 2

In order to become more familair with the process of finding the diatonic order of seventh chords, to help train the ear further, and to train the fingers to sense the 1–7–3–5 voicing more easily, learn to play the same sort of exercise in G major, B-flat major, and D-flat major. The more ambitious student might even learn to play the exercise in all the remaining keys, but even if the reader simply learns to play it C, E-flat, G, B-flat, and D-flat, the following chords will have been realized:

C–7	C△7	G7	C∅7
D–7	F△7	Bb7	D∅7
Eb–7	Db△7	F7	F#∅7
E–7	Eb△7	D7	A∅7
F–7	Gb△7	Ab7	B∅7
G–7	Ab△7		
A–7	Bb△7		
Bb–7	G△7		

Of course this doesn't mean that the student is ready to play any of the above chords on call without having to go through the diatonic seventh chord exercise in the key which would produce the desired chord. But it does mean that the student has at least one way to **find** any of the above chords. Suppose, for example, the player wished to locate an F#∅7 chord. By remembering that the ∅7 chord is found on VII, he/she could quickly figure that if F# is VII then the key is G, finger (but don't play) a G major seventh chord, move each note down one step in the key of G, then play the F#∅7 chord. The ear can also help one to find the chords, with a little trial and error, as it doesn't take long for the ear to begin to recognize any of the four chord qualities taken up thus far, especially since only one voicing is being used.

The II-V-I Progression

II-7 V7 to I $^\Delta$7 is by far the most common sequence of chords in existence, comprising 70-100% of the chords found in most tunes. Sometimes the presence of these chords are disguised by frequent modulations to other keys, but if you can recognize the presence of the new key and go on analyzing the progression in terms of Roman numeral functions (adopting the new keynote as I), the presence of the II-V-I progression will quickly become obvious. In fact, whole tunes have been written which use nothing other than that progression. The order is nearly always the same, too. I seldom leads to V or II, II seldom leads to I, and V seldom leads to II. Furthermore the chord-types are nearly always the same. II and V are never major seventh chords, V is almost never a minor seventh chord (unless it is being used as II of IV), I is only a dominant seventh chord in a blues, or if it is really functioning as V7 of IV. Instead the order and the chord types are nearly always II-7, V7, and I$^\Delta$ 7. The II-V progression is slightly more common than II-V-I, because: (1) composers like to avoid overusing the tonic chord (I); (2) because there is also a minor seventh chord on III, sometimes the progression will be extended to III-7, VI7 (an altered chord, as a secondary dominant), II-7, V7, I, creating the sound of an extra II-V; (3) sometimes the II-V is repeated several times before going to I, as in "Speak Low" or "Tea For Two" or "That Old Black Magic"; (4) the II-V progression often 'side-slips' through several 'keys' before landing on a chord that could be called I, especially in bebop tunes, like "Blues For Alice", "Groovin' High", "Moment's Notice", or "Lazybird".

At any rate, we need to be prepared to play a great number of II-V and II-V-I progressions. Consider, however, the problem of playing successive chords often and quickly that are so far apart in the scale. Each entails leaping up a fourth interval or down a fifth interval, in either case about a half an octave! If we use the 1-7-3-5 vocing exclusively, it would look like this, in the of C:

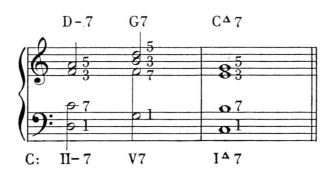

FIGURE 12

Although the 1-7-3-5 voicing sounds good when playing isolated chords and chords running up a scale (like Exercises 1 and 2), it doesn't accomodate the II-V or II-V-I progression very gracefully. The problems are: (1) the hands have to move too far: (2) because of the excessive motion of the hands, the eyes will probably have to leave the music page in order to move to the right place for the next chord; (3) the voicings will not sound smoothly-connected; and (4) the V7 chord sounds a little stark, bland, uninteresting. To solve all of the foregoing problems, a slight adjustment needs to be made in the voicing formula.

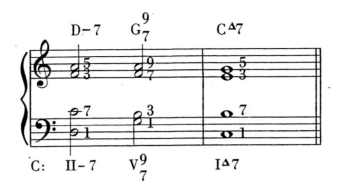

FIGURE 13

If the II-V-I progression is played the way it shows in Figure 13, the hands do not have far to move (in fact, only two **fingers** in the left hand need to move at all), the eyes need not be involved, once the player is accustomed to the feel of the voicings, the voicings sound smoothly-connected (the notes in the right hand don't move anywhere and the top note in the left hand incorporates the logical and common resolution of the 7th of the II chord (C) to the 3rd of the V chord (B), and the V chord now has a 9th added to it, causing it to sound a little more dressed up. Note how the 5th of the V chord was omitted, in order to keep the number of chord notes at four. The fifth of most chords is reasonably dispensable, compared to other chord members. The new voicing formula for the II-V-I progression actually only affects the V chord, as the II and I remain 1-7-3-5- voicings. Study the motion of the II-V-I voicing shown in Figure 13 (especially the motion of II to V), so it can be more easily reproduced in other keys. The II is played as its usual 1-7-3-5. When going to the V chord, retain **both** notes of the II chord that were being played with the right hand, move the top note of the left hand down one half-step (always), and bring the bottom note up a perfect fourth interval (or simply, to the root of the V chord, which is the letter name for the V chord). Then play the I as the usual 1-7-3-5- voicing. Next, practice the motion of the left hand by itself, especially II to V. It will sound more graceful if different fingers are used for the V chord, and since some of the readers are 'three-fingered trumpet players' and 'two-fisted trombone players', it would help to practice the finger exchange of the left hand when going from II to V.

LEFT HAND

(numbers in parenthesis are **finger** numbers, **not** chord members)

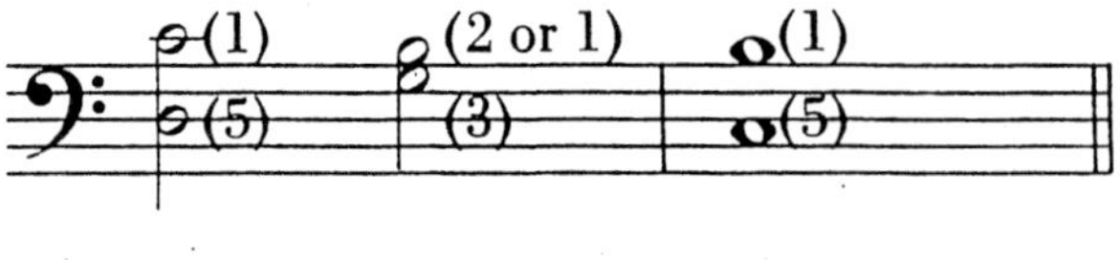

FIGURE 14

For the student who is less familiar with the keyboard and/or reading bass clef notation, Figure 15 shows the II-V-I motion of the left hand in relation to the keyboard.

LEFT HAND

Plain (unparenthesied) numbers are the fingers used for the II chord. The parenthesied numbers are the fingers used when going to the V chord. The fingers for the I chord do not show here.

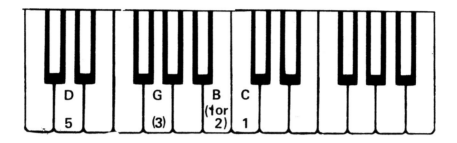

FIGURE 15

The left hand motion of the II-V voicing should be practiced alone until the motion is familiar, comfortable, and can be executed without thinking and without looking at the hand. Practice this in all keys, as the motion will feel slightly different when black keys are involved. When the motion is sufficiently ingrained, the student will find that playing a II-V progression is as easy as playing II by itself, which is like having two chords under one roof, and considering how often the II-V will be encountered, using the II-V voicing formula should prove most beneficial. The I chord is easily learned in all keys because it uses only notes of the familiar major scale. Therefore it is easy to add the I chord to the II-V's, giving the player a **three-chord** progression that is easily-played and extremely common.

The left hand voicing formula for the II-V can be heard in many bebop pianists, like Bud Powell and Horace Silver, as accompaniment to their right hand solos. Sometimes they even applied that motion to a long series of **only** dominant seventh chords (in other words, no minor seventh chords), especially when the dominants moved around the cycle of fifths (or circle of keys). In the early 1950's Horace Silver played the chords shown in Figure 16 a number of times on Miles Davis' recording of "Old Devil Moon". Notice that the right hand is actually descending in half-steps while the left hand moves around the cycle of fifths. Although we haven't yet been introduced to the particular added and altered chord notes (13, +9) used here by Silver, it is obvious that the motion of the two hands causes two types of dominants to alternate evenly (13, +9, 13, +9, etc.)

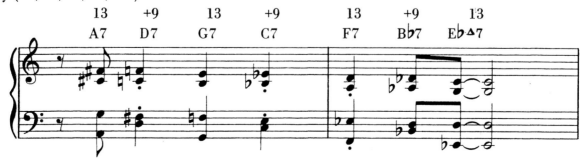

FIGURE 16

The II-V voicing formula can also be applied to other types of chords, if they are located the same distance apart as the II and V. For example, it is fairly common to encounter the I$^\triangle$7 to IV$^\triangle$7 progression, like the 3rd and 4th bars of "Autumn Leaves". Figure 17 shows how this application is played.

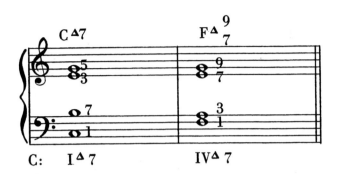

FIGURE 17

The II-V and II-V-I progressions now need to be practiced profusely, until they can be played with little hesitation, in any key. At this point it should be mentioned that the primary task is to become quick with laying the hands on the II chords, since going to the V has been made easy and the I chord will always be relatively easier to find and also occurs a little less frequently. One thing to notice is that minor seventh chords (II function) on D, E, and A only involve white keys, and the E-flat minor seventh uses only black keys. The student who remembers this will be able to find minor seventh chords in those keys more quickly, and those four keys comprise 25% of the total number to be learned. C and F major sevenths are also all white keys.

One very helpful way to learn all the II-V's is to play each key repeatedly (i.e., D-7 to G7, D-7, G7, etc., ad infinitum) until it is being played accurately and with little thought or effort, **then** move the progression up a half- step (E♭-7 and A♭7) and repeat that key interminably until it is easy, then move up another half-step and so on, until all keys have been played in this manner. To make this project enjoyable, I usually have my classes comp the II-V in a sort of latin montuno feeling, similar to Figure 18 (below), to which I will add a bass line in the same rhythmic feeling or improvise against their comping. When I hear that everyone is playing that key correctly, I count two measures out loud as a signal (they continue playing all the while) after which everyone shifts up another half-step.

FIGURE 18

After the montuno exercise with the II-V's, then go through all keys, playing each key **four consecutive** times before going on to the next key, then cut it down to two times in each key, and finally **only once in** every key. Start with slower tempos and gradually increase the tempo each round of keys.

The next step is to practice II-V's and II-V-I's in modulating patterns that simulate the patterns found in tunes. Many tunes modulate down in whole steps, like "How High The Moon", "Solar", "Tune-up", and "Laura". Exercise 3 and Exercise 4 both modulate in such a pattern. After practicing them alone, try to obtain a copy of Volume 1 and Volume 3 of Jamey Aebersold's **A New Approach To Jazz Improvisation.** You will find that the last track on side 2 of Volume 1 is exactly the same as the progression Exercise 3 of this book, and the first track on side 1 of Volume 3 is the same as Exercise 4 in this book. You can turn the balance knob of your record player and eliminate the piano track, so that you can supply the piano comping and enjoy having bass and drum accompaniment. It would also be a good idea to occasionally listen to the piano track on the record, though, to help with learning to comp better. Aebersold also has a separately-sold book (in addition to the book that comes with each of the play-along records) which has written transcriptions of everything Aebersold played (on piano) on Volume 1. Since Aebersold (who is actually a saxophonist) comps extraordinarily well, better than most pianists, these transcriptions have proven to be extremely valuable, especially to pianists who can read, but have trouble with comping effectively. It is also a good lesson in voicing economy, as Aebersold uses very few different voicings, but uses them so well, that the listener/player is not aware of the economy. He is using rootless voicings exclusively, which are not taken up until later in this book, but the student can still study the comping rhythms used in the meantime.

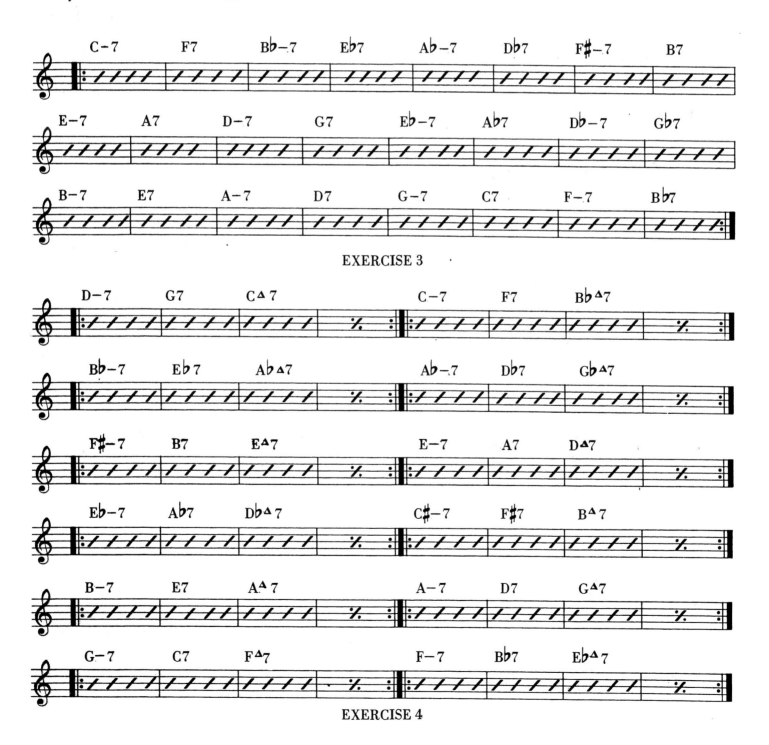

EXERCISE 3

EXERCISE 4

Two other tracks in Volumes 1 and 3 of Aebersold's series that would be helpful at this time are Volume 1, the last track on side 1 ("Four Measure Cadences"), which is a series of II-V-I's in six of the more common keys, and Volume 3, Side 1, Track 2 ("Random II-V's"), which is a track of II-V's in all keys, in a random order (the books that come with the records show the progressions for each of the tracks).

The student should be cautioned not to start near the top of the keyboard when playing a long, descending sequence of keys, just to keep from having to change octaves in mid-stream. Also avoid starting in the middle of the keyboard and continuing downward in keys to a point where the chords are being played in a range that is so low on the keyboard that they sound muddy. The 1-7-3-5 sounds best in the middle and lower middle range. If it is played too high, it sounds 'tinny' (like a celeste), and if it is played too low, it becomes muddy and unclear. The answer lies in not being afraid to change octaves when necessary. Naturally, the non-pianist is reluctant to change octaves bcause the tendency, at first, is not to think so much of each chord's structure and identity, but simply to remember which finger goes where, in relation to the last chord or key played. This approach is all right, at first, but eventually the student must be ready to change octaves more willingly and not to feel helpless if the modulation sequence is not so orderly, as will be the case in many tune's progressions.

When it is no longer difficult to play a II-V or a II-V-I in any key, which takes much less time than one might think, depending upon the individual's investment of practice time, then it is time to start reading the progressions to various tunes, concentrating first on tunes which use virtually nothing but II-V's and II-V-I's throughout. Examples of such tunes are "Tune-Up", "Solar", "Autumn Leaves", "How High The Moon", "Pent-up House", "Laura", "Peace", "Gone With The Wind", "It's You Or No One.", "Everything Happens To Me", and "You Are Too Beautiful".

As stated earlier, chord symbols on lead sheets are given in **lettered** symbols, rather than Roman mumerals. This means that until the player is accustomed to recognizing a II-V or II-V-I in lettered symbols, he/she may pass up many opportunities to apply the easily rendered voicings for those progressions. It would be helpful, then, to have some means by which those progressions can be quickly recognized. First of all, study and memorize the circle of fifths, shown in Figure 19. The II-V and II-V-I progressions agree with that circle, in small slices, also shown in Figure 19.

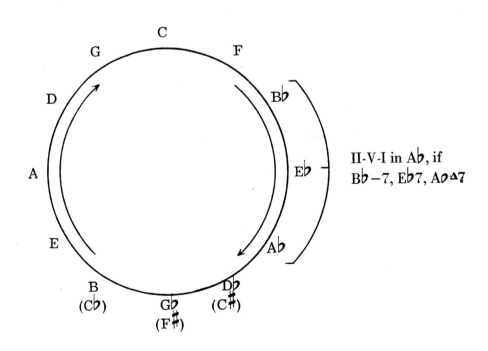

FIGURE 19

Secondly, look at the **types** of chords encountered, as II will nearly always be a minor seventh chord, V will always be a dominant seventh chord, and I will nearly always be a major seventh chord (unless it is appearing in a blues or as I in a **minor** key), and the three chords will nearly always be in the same sequence (II, then V, then I) Get into the habit of suspecting that a minor seventh chord will be a II, then check the next chord and see if it is a dominant seventh chord whose root is one letter forward in the cycle of fifths, and check to see if the next chord is a major seventh chord whose root is one more letter forward in the cycle. In time, one begins to recognize the three chords as common companions, regardless of the particular key. Also be ready to translate the letter enharmonically, in case the person who prepared the lead sheet writes something like Db–7, F♯7, Cb▲7, or C♯–7, Gb7, B▲7, both of which are II-V-I progressions in B major or C-flat major, but clumsily written. Expect to see a lot of II-V's that don't go to I, instead perhaps, going to another II-V. Also, don't be deceived by added notes and alterations, which may catch the eye, but which may not actually change the function of the chord, like a V7 that has an added ninth or thirteenth, or a I chord that might have an added sixth, ninth, or raised fourth.

When reading the chord progression to any tune, there will probably be at least one or two problem areas, like a 'surprise' chord that doesn't quite fit into an otherwise logical sequence, or a place where the player simply has to lift the hands and move to a chord that might be distantly removed from the preceding chords. Chances are, those places are the only places in the progression which cause it to be distinctive, interesting and imaginative, without which the progression might sound pretty dull.

Read the following progressions enough times to be able to play them in a steady tempo without faltering. These are chord progressions to actual tunes, though they don't bear titles.

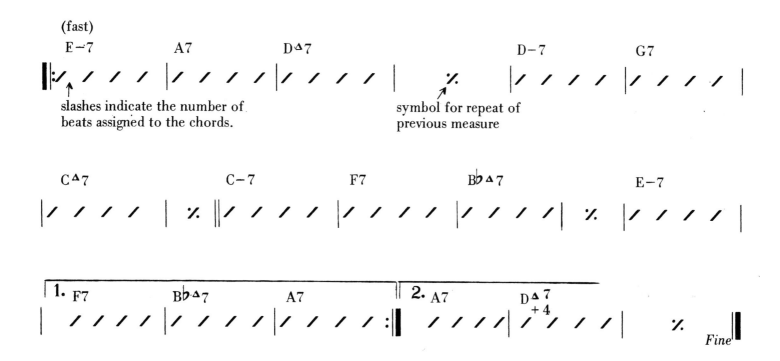

PROGRESSION 1

(the student may want to bracket the II-V's and II-V-I's for awhile, until such time as they can be recognized without marking the sheet)

In order to play the last chord of Progression 1, which has a raised fourth added, simply lower the top note of the 1-7-3-5 voicing from A (the fifth) to G♯ (the +4), omitting the fifth altogether.

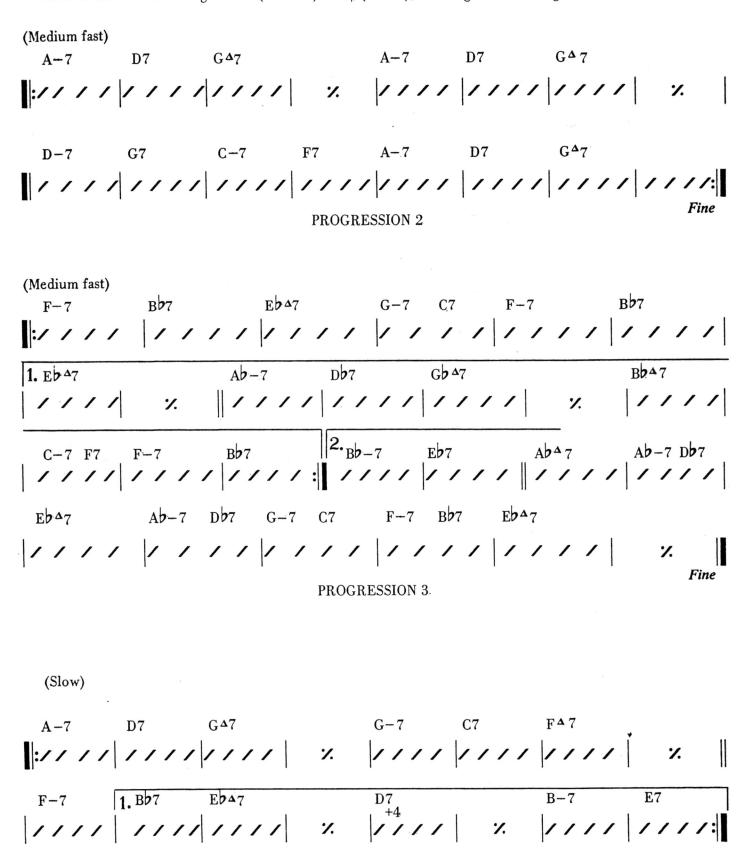

PROGRESSION 2

PROGRESSION 3.

PROGRESSION 4

Before going on to the next set of progressions, we need to expand on the harmonic knowledge presented thus far. Up to now, only **major** keys have been in use, though many tunes are in minor, and many tunes that are chiefly in the major mode will have portions that are in a minor key. The II chord in minor keys is usually a half-diminished seventh chord, instead of a minor seventh chord. It will be remembered that the half-diminished seventh chord was the chord type found on VII in Exercises 1 and 3. It was pointed out in Figure 9 that the alternate name for that chord is a minor seventh chord with a flatted fifth, therefore all that needs to be done to a minor seventh chord to make it become a half-diminished seventh chord is to lower its fifth. In the 1-7-3-5 voicing, the fifth is on top, hence a minor seventh chord becomes a half-diminished seventh chord when we lower the top note of the voicing by one-half step.

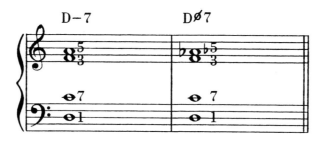

FIGURE 20

The half-diminished chord still functions as II, but II of a **minor** key. The V7 chord in a minor key usually an **altered** ninth in it, either a lowered ninth (♭9) or a raised or augmented ninth (+9 or ♯9). The fifth of the V7 in minor is usually raised, also, (+5 or ♯5) but the fifth has been omitted from the II-V formula presently in use, so it doesn't matter, for the moment.

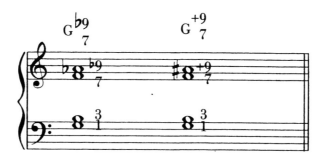

FIGURE 21

The I chord in a minor key is, of course, a minor chord, and may appear in a variety of forms, left to the discretion of the player. In a simple song in minor, it is sometimes best to omit any sort of seventh, leaving it as a 3-note chord (a triad), like the first voicing given in Figure 22. Some jazz pianists will use a minor seventh chord on I, just like the type normally used on II in a major key. For general purposes, however, it is recommended that the student use either the minor sixth chord (the third voicing shown in Figure 22) or the minor-major seventh chord (the last voicing in Figure 22).

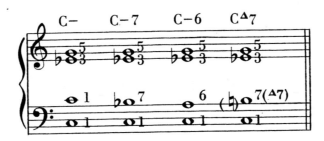

FIGURE 22

Figure 23 combines the three chords (II-V-I in minor) in the form that is recommended for general use, though the student should learn some of the alternate forms (shown in Figures 21 and 22) for purposes of variety and in those cases where the chord symbols for the tune dictate a particular form of I.

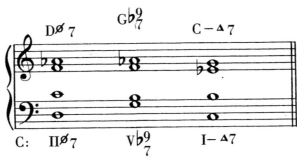

FIGURE 23

Use Exercise 5 for practicing the II-V-I progression in minor. This progression is the same sequence used in Aebersold's Volume 3, track 4, on side 1, should the student wish to practice the exercise in tempo with bass and drum accompaniment.

EXERCISE 5

Although the V7 chord in the II-V voicing formula includes a ninth, the II and I chords do not. Since adding the ninth to these two chords would make them more interesting in sound, perhaps now is the time to add them. A ninth can be added on top of either or both chords, or it can be worked into the middle of the voicing (adjacent to the third) for 'bite'. Both are shown in Figure 24 and both should be practiced. Note that when the ninth of the II chord is retained for the V chord it causes the V chord to have a thirteenth, which causes it to become more interesting, also. To practice the new chord members of Figure 24 in all keys, re-use Exercises 3 and 4, with or without the Aebersold play-along record.

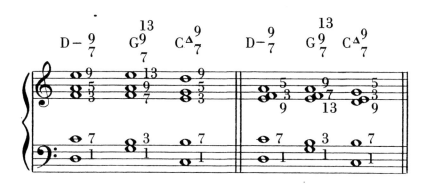

FIGURE 24

Finally, before reading the progressions to more tunes, it would be helpful to see how the 1-7-3-5 voicing may be permutated to fit **any** type of needed chord, even some that have not yet been presented. Figure 25 shows this flexibility.

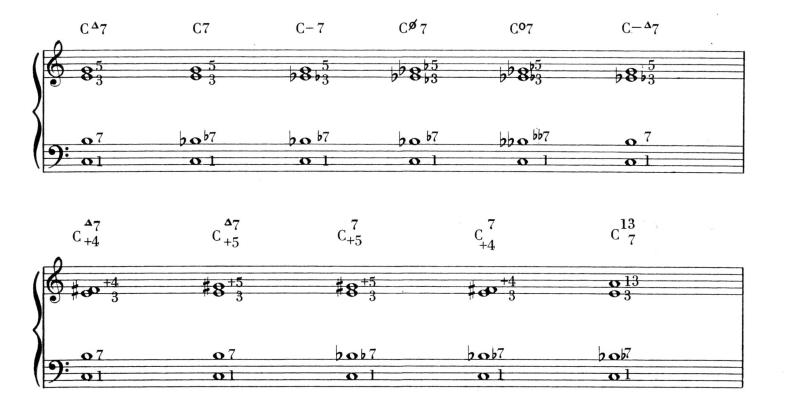

FIGURE 25

Bear in mind that Figure 25 includes only the flexibility of the 1-7-3-5 voicing without adding a fifth or sixth note to that four-note voicing. All but one of the chords could have had a ninth added to it. Four of them could have had either a raised or lowered ninth. Six of them could have had an added thirteenth.

Now the student, after practicing and studying Figures 23-25 and the suggested exercises, is ready to cope with tunes which use II-V-I in minor and tunes which use diminished seventh chords (°7) and altered or added-to chords, plus being able to add ninths to II and I chords and thirteenths to V chords at will. From this point on, the student should use his/her own discretion about using ninths and thirteenths. It might be helpful to review Progressions 1-4 to practice adding those chord extensions. The following series of progressions (5-11) will contain some of the new items taken up since Progressions 1-4.

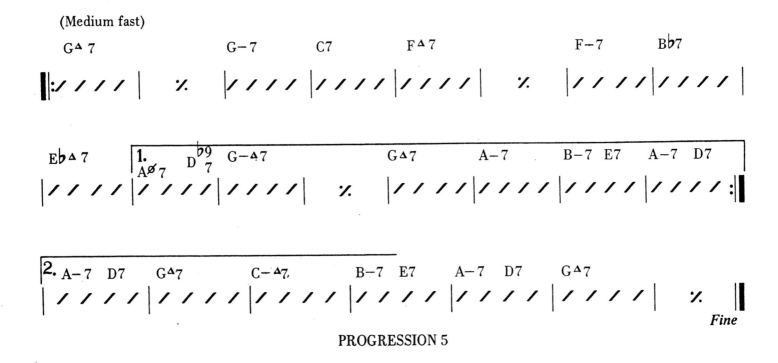

PROGRESSION 5

PROGRESSION 6

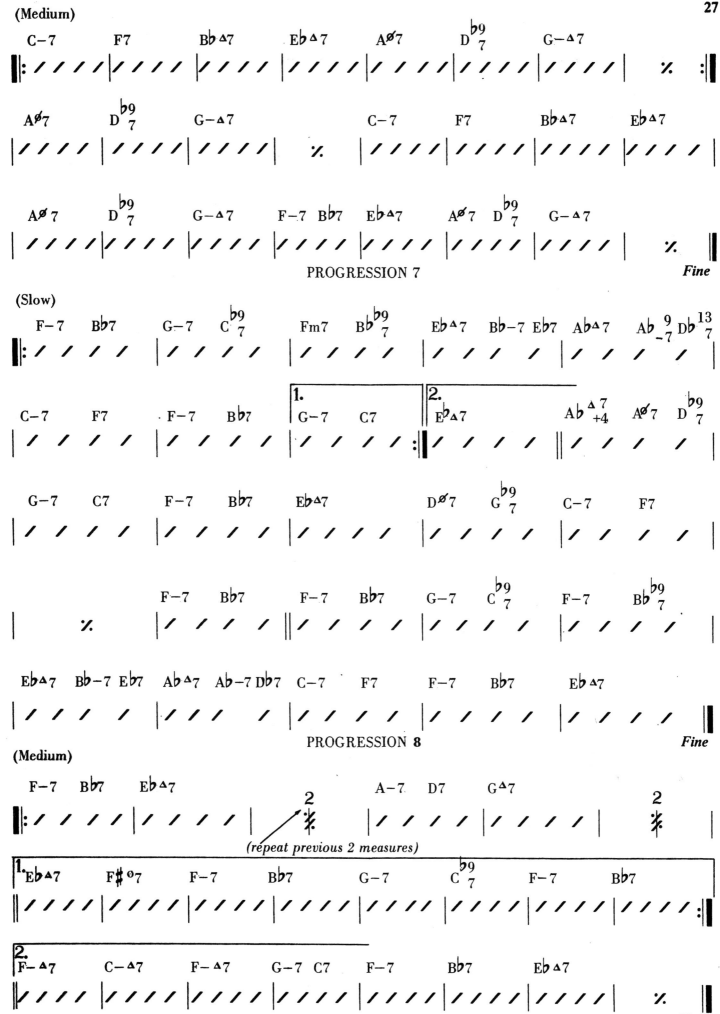

PROGRESSION 7

PROGRESSION 8

PROGRESSION 9

(Slow)

$C-_7^9$ F_7^{13} Bb△7 G-7 C-7 F7 Dø7 G7 C-7 Ab7 D-7 G7

$\|: / / / / \,|\, / / / / \,|\, / / / / \,|\, / / / / \,|\, / / / / \,|\, / / / / \,|$

C-7 F7 **1.** D-7 G7 **2.** Bb△7 F-7 Bb_7^{+9} Eb△7 C7 Fø7 Bb_7^{b9}

$|\, / / / / \,|\, / / / / \,:\|\, / / / / \,\|\, / / / / \,|\, / / / / \,|\, / / / / \,|$

Eb△7 Eø7 A_7^{+9} D△7 G-7 C7 C-7 F7 $C-_7^9$ F_7^{13}

$|\, / / / / \,|\, / / / / \,|\, / / / / \,|\, / / / / \,|\, / / / / \,\|\, / / / / \,|$

$Bb△_7^9$ G-7 C-7 F7 Dø7 G_7^{b9} C-7 Ab7 D-7 G7 C-7 F7 Bb△7

$|\, / / / / \,|\, / / / / \,|\, / / / / \,|\, / / / / \,|\, / / / / \,|\, / / / / \,|\, / / / / \,|\, / / / / \,\|$

PROGRESSION 10

Fine

(Slow)

Aø7 D_7^{b9} G-7 C7 B△7 Cø7 F_7^{+9} Bb△7 B-7 E7 A△7 F#-7

$\|: / / / / \,|\, / / / / \,|\, / / / / \,|\, / / / / \,|\, / / / / \,|\, / / / / \,|$

Ebø7 Ab_7^{b9} Db△7 Cø7 $B+4^{7}$ Bb△7

$|\, / / / / \,|\, / / / / \,|\, / / / / \,|\, / / / / \,:\|$

PROGRESSION 11

Before completing our work with the 1-7-3-5 voicings, several items need to be mentioned: melody-playing, improvisation, and expansion of the 1-7-3-5 voicing. With regard to melody-playing, bear in mind that only two fingers of the right hand are occupied with playing the chord (unless, of course, ninths are added to the II and I chords). Therefore three fingers are available for playing melodies. Two problems will be encountered when attempting this; the fact that the melody will sometimes move upward, out of reach from the chord voicing, and at other times the melody will descend into the voicing. To solve the problem of the upward melody, either use the pedal to sustain the chord after the attack and reach up (with the right hand) to play the melody, or move the whole voicing up an octave so that the melody is still within reach, or leave out the right hand notes of the chord in order to play the melody (especially if the melody is running up at least several notes of the chord, anyway). To solve the problem of the melody which descends into the chord voicing, either move the whole voicing down an octave or leave out the right hand notes of the voicing (especially if the melody is running down several notes of the chord).

As for improvisation, remember that many bebop pianists used the somewhat bare sound of the root and seventh in the left hand (or root and third, in the case of the V chord of a II-V situation), since the improvising right hand will probably 'fill-in' other notes of the chord (i.e. the third of the chord) somewhere within the improvised line. If the pianist has large hands and/or long fingers, the left hand can actually play a very effective accompaniment of three notes by playing a 1-7-3 voicing. Horace Silver has used such a voicing. It is illustrated in Figure 26. Note that when going to the V chord, the seventh of the II-7 still resolves to the third of the V chord, but the bottom note of the II chord is retained to become the fifth of the dominant (V), requiring less motion.

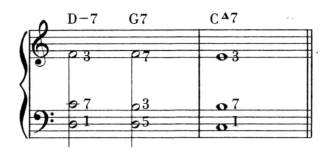

FIGURE 26

Finally, with respect to the possible expansion of the 1-7-3-5 voicing, the voicing could be used as a foundation for an added-to or altered chord, using the remaining fingers of the right hand to accomplish same, as shown in Figure 27 (which illustrates only a **few** of the possibilities).

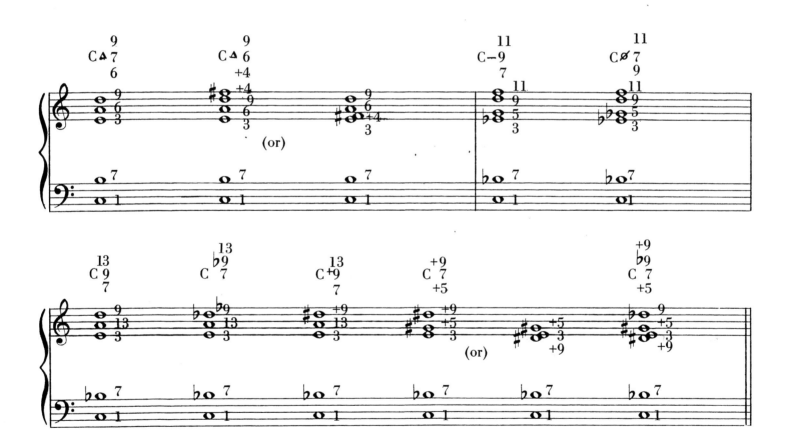

FIGURE 27

The Blues and an Introduction to Rootless Voicings

Simultaneous with learning an important segment of jazz, the blues progression, we will also be learning our first rootless voicings. The 1-7-3-5 voicing that has been stressed up to this point has its advantages in learning basic chord structures, but except in ballad playing, rootless voicings are much more commonplace in the playing of most modern pianists. Leaving out the root causes the chords to sound less fundamental, more modern (because there are likely to be more added and altered chord tones), and the right hand is free to play melodies, improvisation, or to add even more chordal colors, since the rootless voicings are played in the left hand alone. Rootless voicings are also less inhibiting to the bass player, as he doesn't have to worry about playing the root in exactly the same intonation as the pianists' lowest note (if it is the root), he is free to play a scalar line, and the pianist's lowest notes are generally above the register played by the bassist. Incidentally, when using rootless voicings, the lowest note should stay above the C below Middle C to avoid becoming muddy. In other words it should be used in a higher range than the 1-7-3-5 voicing.

Since the traditional blues can be played with only three chords, all of which are dominant seventh chords (even on I!), it makes a good vehicle for learning rootless voicings and for starting to improvise with the right hand. Progression 12 is the traditional, typical 12-bar blues, with rootless voicings given. Progression 12a is the same progression as Progression 12, but the rootless voicings are in a different inversion. There are two inversions for all rootless voicings, one with the seventh on the bottom and the other with the third on the bottom. Both are needed to assure smooth connection, as can be seen by the inversion change between the first and second chords of both Progression 12 and 12a, where the G7 goes to C7.

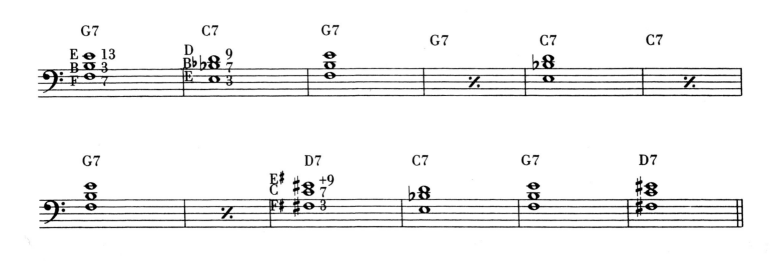

PROGRESSION 12

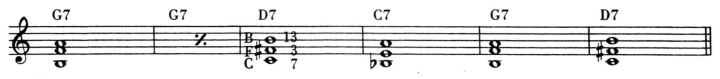

PROGRESSION 12 a

Looking at Progressions 12 and 12a, note the following:

(1) they are in the key of G;

(2) because their ranges are different, one has been written in bass clef and the other in treble clef;

(3) both are to be played by the left hand alone;

(4) the progression is 12 measures in length;

(5) only three chords were needed - G7, C7, and D7;

(6) the progression should be felt in 3 four-bar segments;

(7) the progression could and should be memorized;

(8) the progression can be played at any tempo;

(9) the D7 in the twelfth bar is there only for the purpose of leading into additional choruses. The very last chorus would stay on the G7 chord for **both** the eleventh and twelfth bars;

(10) only three chord voicings are used for each progression;

(11) only three notes are used in each voicing;

(12) the bottom two notes in all voicings are the seventh and third (or third and seventh) of the chord;

(13) each voicing has an added or altered note on top, either a ninth, an augmented (raised) ninth, or a thirteenth;

(14) by shifting inversions (i.e., between the first and second bar of either progression) the chord voicings remained very close together, though their unplayed roots are a fourth or a fifth interval apart;

(15) in both sets of voicings, the bottom two notes go down a half-step to go from G7 (I) to C7 (IV), and they go up a half-step to go from G7 (I) to D7 (V).

Now play Progressions 12 and 12a. First play the voicings with the **right** hand and play the roots of the chords (in a low register) with the left hand, to help the ear to adjust to what it is supposed to perceive or imagine when hearing rootless voicings. Then play the voicings with the left hand alone, in tempo. Volume 2 of the Aebersold series has a slow blues in G on it, with a progression identical to Progressions 12 and 12a, if the student wishes to play with bass and drums and/or listen to a good pianist comp the blues for inspiration.

A peculiar phenomenon becomes possible if only the bottom two notes are played in Progression 12 or 12a. In bar 1 we think of the B as being the third of the G7 and the F is the seventh, and when the bass (root) is added (either by a bass player or by the pianist playing the root with the left hand and playing the B and F wth the right hand), we are satisfied that the voicing really sounds like a G7. Yet if **D-flat** is played in the bass register against the B and F, it sounds like a D♭7! This happens because F is the third of the D-flat chord and B (actually C♭) is the seventh. In other words, dominant sevenths that are a tri-tone (three whole-steps) apart, like G and D-flat, share the same third and seventh, though their names are reversed; that is, F is the seventh of the G chord, but it is the third of the D-flat chord, and B is the third of the G chord, but it is the seventh of the D-flat chord. In fact, both Progressions 12 and 12a in their entirety could become blues progressions in D-flat instead of G, if only the bottom two notes of each voicing are played and if the bass notes are thought of, heard, or played as a D-flat blues (The root sequence would then be: D♭, G♭, D♭, D♭, G♭, G♭, D♭, D♭, A♭, G♭, D♭, A♭). This should help explain why jazz performers will frequently use a device called **tri-tone substitution**, in which they might play a D♭7 in place of a G7. The top notes of the blues voicings were omitted from the explanation of this phenomenon **only** because some of them were inappropriate to the blues style, though they still function as good added or altered tones for another situation. Some players leave out the top tones of the voicings much of the time when playing the blues, since the improvising right hand can supply added and altered chord notes, when needed. Incidentally, the tri-tone experiment described, in which the bass notes were changed from the key of the G to the key of D-flat for Progressions 12 and 12a, could also have been done with the right hand's improvisation; that is, if the player is hearing and playing in the key of D-flat in the right hand, the listener will also perceive a D-flat blues instead of a G blues, if the left hand is only playing the bottom two notes of each voicing.

Adding the improvised right hand will be a challenge to many of the readers, either because he/she doesn't understand the craft of improvisation or simply because it is sometimes difficult to play chord voicings in the left hand while attempting to create an independently flowing right hand (like rubbing the stomach with one hand and patting the head with the other). The following suggestions may help the student to get under way:

(1) learn the responsibilities of the left hand first, thoroughly ingraining the voicings and the progression (through repetition) until the left hand can be put on 'automatic pilot', before adding the right hand;

(2) lean on the blues scale in the right hand for awhile (G, B♭, C, C♯, D, F, G), which can be used **throughout** the progression, regardless of which chord is going on. It won't answer all the needs of developing good blues melody, but until the left hand is more automatic, the right hand can wander up and down notes of the blue scale, semi-automatically, at those times when the eyes and mind are distracted by problems in the left hand;

(3) don't feel too much pressure to produce something spectacular with the right hand's improvisation. It will take time. Be contented, for the moment, just to play the right voicings (left hand) in the right measures and getting the right hand to start moving;

(4) use more repetition in the right hand at first, especially of simple, commonplace blues 'licks' (phrases);

(5) listen to blues players, especially pianists, on record, just to get into the mental-emotional groove;

(6) use Aebersold's play-along for comforting company (Vol. 2, "Slow Blues in G")

(7) pick an uncluttered space in your schedule (2:00 to 4:00 a.m., perhaps), get seated at the piano, set a nice, easy tempo for yourself, and play about 100-1000 consecutive choruses. You'll feel better, emotionally, from the therapeutic aspects of playing the blues, and you'll probably be playing them better, too.

Progressions 12 and 12a are representative of a very simple, traditional blues progression. It has endured and will probably always be used by even the most modern jazz player when he/she wants to create a down home, funky blues. But there **are** many, many different progressions, segments of progressions, and chord substitutions that have been used in various recordings of the blues, some of which have become commonplace amidst all performers. There have been blues that were not 12 bars long (i.e. 8-bar, 16-bar, or 24-bar versions) and blues that have been played in time signatures other than 4/4 (i.e., 3/4, 5/4, and 7/4). And of course the blues is played in **any** tempo from very slow to very fast, though the slow blues is the more traditional. The examples that follow will be restricted to progressions which are in 4/4 and have a length of 12 bars. For ease of assimiliation by the student, they are all in the key of G, the key of Progressions 12 and 12a. It will be noted that many of the alternate chord possibilities will affect only a two or four measure segment of the blues progression, rather than changing the entire progressions. For this reason, bar numbers will be used for the following figures to indicate the segment affected, rather than reproduce the **entire** 12-bar progression.

The first variation on the blues progression is that the IV7 (C7) chord is sometimes omitted from the second bar, causing the entire 4-bar (1-4) segment to be I7 (G7). This need not be shown in a figure.

The second variation, shown in Figure 28, is the interpolation of a minor seventh chord (D-7) in the fourth measure. That measure usually functions as a chord or chords that prepare a sort of temporary modulation to IV (C), the chord of the fifth, and sometimes sixth as well, measure of the blues. The arrival of the IV7 (C7) chord in the fifth bar is the most consistent, dependable trait of any 12-bar blues, though the chord-type may be changed to, say, a C minor seventh chord or a C major seventh chord. Once in a while someone will even find a suitable substitute for the C chord of the fifth and sixth measures, especially B♭-7 and/or E♭7 (♭III−7 and ♭VI7 in the G blues), but it is a rare occurrence and it still points to the tendency of the blues to want to leave the I chord and go to a temporary, contrasting place on the fifth measure. This means that if there is to be a measure of preparation for the fifth bar's contrasting chord or key (be it IV7 or not), it will take place in the fourth measure. So the D-7 chord in the first half of measure 4 in Figure 28 functions as a II chord to the new 'key' of C, and the G7 in the second half of that bar functions (momentarily) as V7 of C, instead of I7 in G.

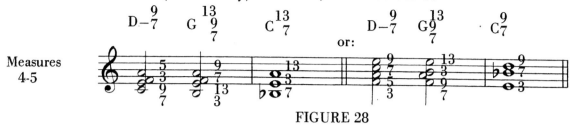

FIGURE 28

Figure 29 shows another common chord substitution for the fourth bar of a blues. This illustrates the use of **tri-tone substitution**, mentioned earlier on page 31, in which on the added tone (top note of the three-note voicing) indicates (aurally) that D♭7 is being implied by the voicing, instead of G7. Of course the bassist **might** play D♭, and the pianist' improvising right hand will probably use notes that will reinforce the change from G7 to D♭7. But it is also true that the top notes of the voicings (especially the D♯, which would function like a raised fifth to a G chord) are so inappropriate to the expected sound of a I7 chord in the blues that the listener already senses a possible change of chord root. It is probably obvious to the reader, also, that a D♭7 leads into the C7 as well as a G7 leads to C7, in terms of the **sound** (smooth).

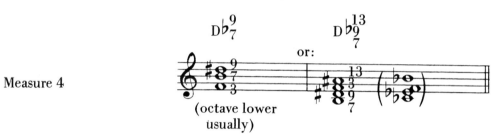

FIGURE 29

Figure 30 shows a slightly different way to handle a tri-tone substitution in the fourth bar of a blues. We simply add a II function (A♭-7) in front of the D♭7 chord, just as we did in Figure 28, where a measure of G7 became D-7 and G7 (two beats each). Now that D♭7 is substituting for G7, it too can have a II function in the first half of the measure.

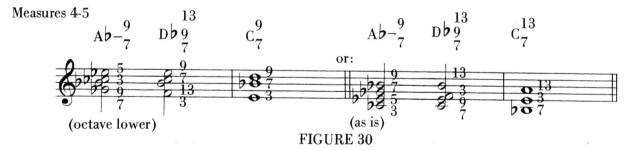

FIGURE 30

The IV7 of the fifth bar of the blues establishes the new 'home (C) away from home' (G). If the sixth bar is **not** a continuation of the duration of the C7, it will probably contain a chord or chords which will self-destruct the new 'key' of the fifth bar and/or push the progression toward the original I (G). Several possibilities for the sixth bar are shown in Figure 31.

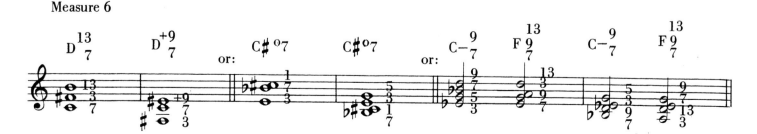

FIGURE 31

If the blues is a **minor** blues, say a G minor blues, then it is probable that all G chords will be minor chords, except, possibly, for the fourth measure (where G7 might be used to prepare for the C chord), and the C chords will probably all be minor chords, and the chord of the sixth bar is more likely to be a continuance of the C minor chord, though sometimes the sixth bar of a G minor blues will have an F7 (natural sequel to a C-7 chord) or a D7 (which leads back to G minor).

Although the seventh and eighth bars of the blues are usually a I function (like G7), sometimes a B-7 (III-7) is substituted for I (G), since they sound much alike, and whether or not the B-7 chord appears in the seventh measure, an E7 chord is commonly used in the eighth measure, either to prepare the final cadence (bars 9-12, especially 9 and 10), or as a natural sequel to the B-7 chord (as in III-7 to VI7, which is like II-7 to V7, though a whole-step higher). This is shown in Figure 32.

Measures 7-8

FIGURE 32

Note that Figures 28-32 provide the same progression twice within the figure, but in two different voicings. The player should choose the voicing that connects best with the preceding and following chord voicings, or simply the voicing that is closest to the preceding voicing.

If an E7 (VI7) appears in the eighth measure, the ninth measure will probably be A-7(II-7), A7(II7), or Eb7 (bVI7), as shown in Figure 33. Sometimes an A-7 is used in the ninth measure, even if there is **not** an E7 in the eighth measure. In all three instances the chord of the tenth bar will either be a D7(V7) or a tri-tone substitute for V7 (as in Figure 34).

Measures 8-10

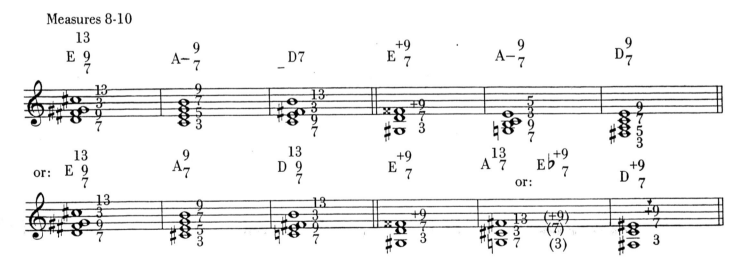

FIGURE 33

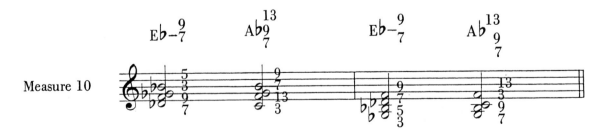

FIGURE 34

Finally, measures 11 and 12, if they are not taken up with the traditional G7(17) and D7(V7) chords shown in Progression 12 and 12a (page 30), will usually contain a **turnaround** or **turnback** (both are terms for brief, quick-moving progression segments, usually found at the end of a tune or one of its sections, and functions as a means to avoid a lull during a long duration of I, as well as to prepare the ear for going on to another section, repeat of a section, or even a new chorus). Figure 35 shows a typical turnaround that might appear in the eleventh and twelfth measures of a blues.

Measures 11-12

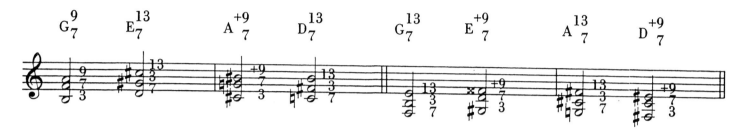

FIGURE 35

Sometimes a four-measure segment (especially bars 1-4) of a blues is revised in such a way that it forms a chain of logical chord motion that consumes the entire four measures, and often should not be interrupted until the four bars have elapsed. Figures 36 and 37 illustrate two plans for the first four measures of a blues. Both plans were used by Charles Parker, among many others.

Measures 1-5

FIGURE 36

Measures 1-5

FIGURE 37

In the course of showing variations on the blues progression, circumstances forced the introduction of rootless voicings for the II-V progression, which will not be taken up until the beginning of Section 2, formally. So if the reader feels overburdened with new voicing information and examples at this time, understand that what is to follow shortly, in Section 2, will reinforce the theory and use of the rootless II-V.

Progression 13 combines **some** of the traits of blues progresssions shown in isolation in Figures 28-37, as one example of many such possibilities.

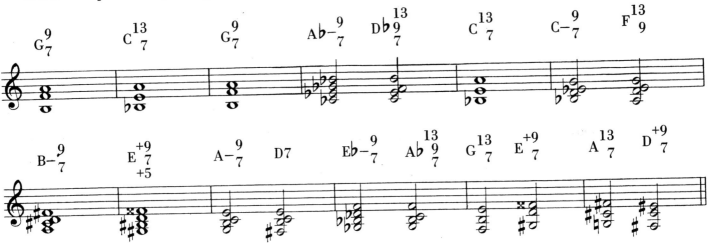

PROGRESSION 13

Blues and blues progression are discussed thoroughly in Chapter 3 of **The Complete Method For Improvisation** [2], Appendix C of **Improvising Jazz** [3], and in David Baker's **Jazz Improvisation.** [4] By purchasing a copy of Aebersold's **Nothin' But Blues** (Volume 2 of the series), you will acquire a group of various blues progressions, from traditional to modern, plus an accompaniment record with which to practice the progressions. Keep looking for even more traits of blues progressions.

When the left hand voicings become relatively automatic, start adding the right hand improvisation. Learn at least several kinds of blues progressions in **all** keys and play them often. In the event that you found a copy of the Aebersold piano-comping transcriptions for Volume 1 (mentioned on page 19), read the transcriptions for the two blues tracks (in F and Bb), study the similarities in the voicing patterns, note the sort of notespacing that can be played with the right hand when not soloing, and study the comping style from a rhythmic point of view.

Some jazz pianists will use the left hand voicings to reinforce a melody-playing or soloing right hand, comping the left hand simultaneously with the accented notes of the melody or solo. Indeed, sometimes a pianist will re-strike the left hand with **every** melody or solo note. At such times, the melody or solo are easier to hear (especially if the player plays the melody or solo in octaves) and have the effect of being louder and more dynamic and rhythmic. Red Garland and Bill Evans are just two examples of the many pianists who have used this approach. It is more likely to occur at the intensity peak of the solo (about 3/4 of the way through the solo, usually), or in the melody chorus, or at anytime in which the drummer and/or bassist are loud enough to endanger the audibility of the piano.

For the more adventurous and practical students, there is one more dimension to be added to the uses of rootless voicings. Often a pianist is confronted with the lack of a bass player, in practice or performance. At such times, the left hand voicings can be played with the **right** hand and the left hand is free to play a walking bass line (usually in quarter-notes). Learn bass line cliches (by listening to bassists on record), transcribe a few bass lines on the blues, and play them alone, with the left hand, for awhile before adding the right hand chords. Imitate (with touch) the sound of a bassist playing a walking line.

END OF SECTION 1

---

[2] - Coker, Studio P/R, Lebanon, Indiana, 1981.

[3] - Coker, Prentice-Hall, Englewood Cliffs, New Jersey, 1964.

[4] - Baker, Maher Publications, Chicago, Illinois, 1969.

The Rootless II-V-I In Major

Figures 28, 30, 31, 32, 33, 34, and 36, as well as Progression 13, all make use of the rootless II-V Some even use II-V-I, but the I in a blues is a dominant seventh chord-type (I7, or G7), and for general purposes we need the I to be a major seventh chord or a minor-major seventh chord (for minor tunes, minor keys). Also, in Section 1 we didn't have the opportunity to discuss and practice the rootless II-V by itself, which is needed, as it was necessary with the l-7-3-5 voicings on the II-V and II-V-I progressions. Again, the voicings need to be practiced until it is almost automatic to do so, so that when our eyes see a chord symbol (or our minds and ears are thinking of a symbol), our response is quick and accurate. And once again, the voicings are typical of what successful jazz pianists have been and are using, therefore worth our while to assimilate.

Comparing Figure 28 with Figure 24, we see a lot of similarity (in addition to the fact that they are II-V-I's in key of C) with respect to the spacing of the chord notes. In fact, if we remove the roots of the D-7 and G7 chords from the voicings in the second half of Figure 24, and compare what remains with the D-7 and G7 chords from the first half of Figure 28, we see that they become identical. The first half of Figure 24 also bears a close resemblance to the second half of figure 28 (don't forget to leave out the roots of Figure 24), the only difference being that one of the voices of each chord in Figure 24 is an octave lower than its counterpart in Figure 28. So in essence, the spacing of rootless voicings is almost identical to the spacing of the two-handed l-7-3-5 voicing (with the ninth added), **except** for the absence of the root.

As there were two inversions of the rootless voicings given for the blues voicings of Section l, so there will be two inversions for the rootless II-V and II-V-I voicings of Section 2. One will have the seventh on the bottom and the other will have the third on the bottom. This will also hold true of the II-V and II-V-I in **minor**. Both inversions are needed for playing tunes, in major and in minor, because we will be frequently confronted with the need to change inversions in order not to move the hand suddenly to a very remote place on the keyboard. Sometimes a change of inversion will be needed in order to get the left hand out of the way of the right hand's activity. Figure 38 shows the two inversions for the rootless II-V-I voicings in C major. Most students find the inversion shown first in Figure 38 to be the easiest to learn first, because the numbers are easier to remember on the starting II chord (3-5-7-9) and because the intervals are all third intervals (no second or fourth intervals) and therefore a little easier for the hands and fingers to sense the chord's spacing. Yet the second set of II-V-I voicings shown in Figure 38 are generally preferred in **sound** over the other set.

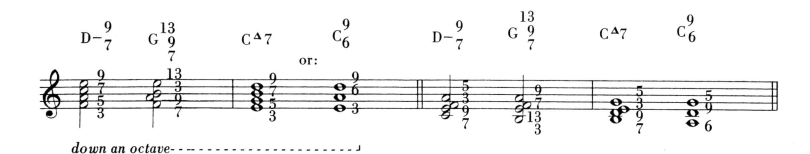

FIGURE 38

It is important for the student to understand that the first segment of Section 2 involves more determination, patience, study, and woodshedding than was necessary in the first segment of Section 1. Suddenly we are confronted with **two** inversions of II-V-I voicings (without the aid of having a root present in the voicing to keep us from getting lost in major, plus the two inversions to be applied also in minor, and all this must be learned very soon in order that we be able to function while reading the progressions to tunes and **applying** those voicings.

In order to learn the new voicings presented in Figure 38, borrow from the activities that were used for learning the 1-7-3-5 voicings of Section 1, namely:

(1) play II-V's (only) in each key, montuno style, repeating that one key until it is mastered or easy, then move the progression up one half-step, continuing the process until all keys have been played, as was done with Figure 18 in Section 1. Then repeat the project, using the other inversion given in Figure 38;

(2) play Exercises 3 and 4 (Section 1, page 19) with the new voicings of Figure 38. Don't forget to use both inversions, going all the way through each exercise with each inversion. If you purchased Aebersold's Volume 1 and 3, play Exercises 3 and 4 with the appropriate play-along track;

(3) play the two Aebersold tracks recommended on page 20 ("Four Measure Cadences" from Volume 1, and "Random II-V's" from Volume 3); and

(4) read Progressions 1-4 (in Section 1, pages 21 & 22), using rootless voicings.

It will be noted in playing tune progressions with rootless voicings that there is a slight problem of a downward drift in the left hand's rootless voicings; that is, you may discover that the hand is a half octave lower by the time you reach the end of eight measures where you might encounter a repeat of the same segment (or at least, the same starting chord symbol). It would make more sense to change inversions at that point, rather than pick up the hand and move it back up a half an octave or more. Two facts cause this downward drift of the left hand. One is that progressions often modulate downward in whole-steps, like progressions 1 and 4. The other is that, because of another common progression sequence, the modulation up a fourth (i.e., going from the key of C to the key of F), we are likely to change inversions at that point (and should!), which contributes to the downward drift. This is shown in Figure 39. Eventually the player will need to move the hand back up to a more reasonable, clear register, perhaps at the end of a section of 8-16 measures, or wherever there is a chord of longer duration, making the change easier.

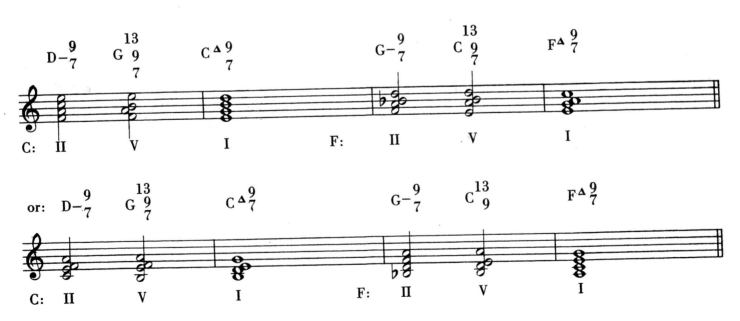

FIGURE 39

Although the downward drift in Figure 39 may seem very slight, the progression segment is only foui measures long, yet the drift has already begun. Add one or two modulations down in whole-steps to the modulation used in Figure 39 and you will see how quickly the hand drifts downward. Because the modulation pattern up a fourth, as shown in the above figure, is extremely common, it provides us with our first reason for needing both inversions. Note that regardless of which inversion is used at the beginning of either of the four-measure progressions shown in Figure 39, it is necessary to change inversions when going from the third chord (C major seventh) to the fourth chord (G minor seventh), if we are to avoid a wide leap. To better prepare the player for these changes of inversion, play Exercise 6 (below), which continues modulating up in fourths all the way around the circle of keys, alternating between the two inversions needed.

Shortly after it is comfortable to play the rootless voicings with the left hand, the right hand should be brought into play. This could be in the form of improvising, playing melodies, and playing patterns. With respect to the latter, take note that most of the Aebersold books, in the early pages, contain many suggested patterns for playing with the record. For example, after learning the left hand voicings for the II-V-I progression in minor, found on the following pages, open your copy of the Aebersold book for Volume 3 and turn to the suggested patterns for Side 1, Track 4, and play them with the right hand while continuing to play the rootless left hand voicings (Aebersold's patterns 9, 11, 12, 13, and 15 are especially choice).

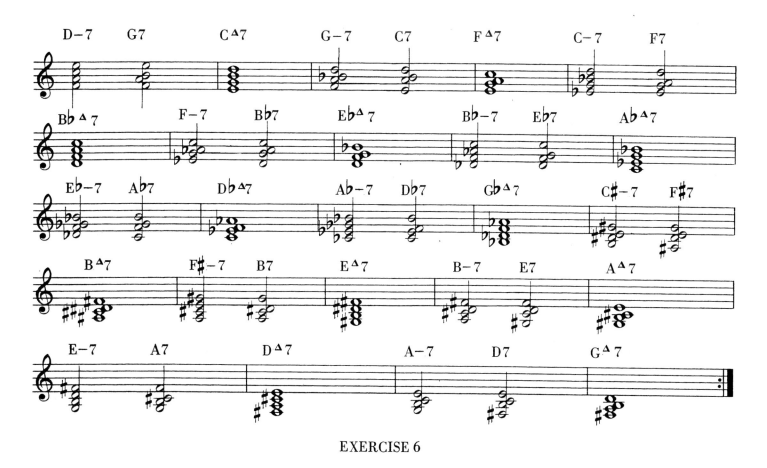

EXERCISE 6

After playing Exercise 6 with the voicings shown there, play the exercise once more, reversing the voicing-inversion sequence; that is, start the exercise with the other inversion of the Dm7 (the **second** Dm7 voicing shown in Figure 39). The first four bars of the exercise (No. 6) will look like the second four-bar sequence in Figure 39. Try to play the rest of the progression symbols in Exercise 6 without writing out the voicings in the manner they were provided in the exercise for the other inversion. All the voicings have been written out so far, **only** to eliminate confusion, not to take away the initiative of the reader or to establish a habit of reading notes. Playing jazz is too spontaneous to permit only the **reading** of chord voicings and symbols — it must all be internalized in time.

To further hone the ability to change inversions, play Exercise 7, which is merely a cycle of dominant seventh chords. Figure 40 shows how to get under way. Note that the exercise should be played twice, reversing the inversion pattern the second time through, as shown in the second part of Figure 40.

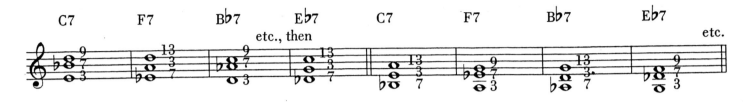

FIGURE 40

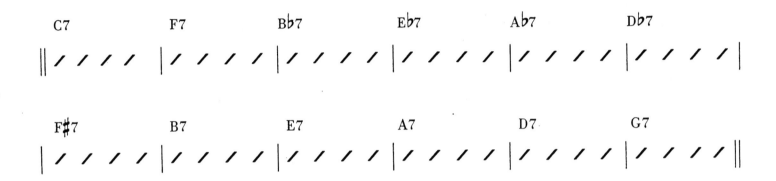

EXERCISE 7

Aebersold has cycles of dominant seventh chords in Volumes 1, 16, and 21, if the student wishes to practice Exercise 7 with bass and drum accompaniment. Also, if a copy of the piano comping transcriptions for Volume 1 was obtained, study the voicings and comping patterns used on the track called "Cycle of Dominants".

The Rootless II-V-I In Minor

In the minor mode, II chords are usually a half-diminished seventh chord instead of a minor seventh chord, V is usually altered to include a raised fifth and a raised ninth instead of being a blander dominant seventh type, and I will be a minor chord of some sort instead of a major seventh chord. The inversions, however, remain the same as II-V-I in major, having either the third or the seventh on the bottom of the voicing. Figure 41 shows both inversions in C minor. Note that there are alternate possibilities given for the II chord, depending upon whether or not the player wants to use the ninth (the ninth sometimes sounds strange to the ear on half-diminished seventh chords, depending on the player and the tune), and alternate voicings for the I chord, also, as there were for II-V-I's in major. These choices are left to the discretion of the player.

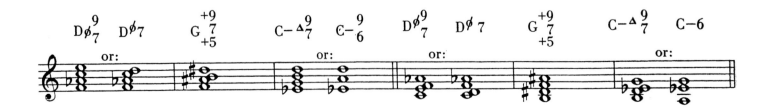

FIGURE 41

Use Exercise 5 (in Section 1) for the practice of II-V-I's in minor, using rootless voicings. Be sure to practice both inversions (see Figure 41). Use the corresponding track in Aebersold's Volume 3 if you wish to work with a rhythm section for your practice of Exercise 5.

When the playing of Exericse 5 can be accomplished without too much strain, then play Progressions 5-11 (in Section 1, pages 26-28), which all involve the use of II-V-I in minor.

Finally, start reading tunes out of fake books, song books, or any source which includes chord symbols and melody, playing the chord with the left hand and playing the melody and improvisation with the right hand. It would also be helpful to learn to add a few notes to the chord in the right hand, since you will probably spend a good portion of your playing time providing accompaniment (comping) for others in the group, and you will want to engage both hands in those situations, using the rootless left hand voicings as a foundation.

Contrapuntal Elaboration of Static Harmony (CESH)

A large percentage of tunes will use a harmonic device called Contrapuntal Elaboration of Static Harmony, which we will call CESH (for obvious reasons!). "Contrapuntal Elaboration" means that one of the chord voices is in motion and "Static Harmony" means that the other notes of the chord are **not** in motion. Although CESH occurs more often in minor, it also is used in major. The moving voice is usually the chord root itself, descending in half-steps while the other notes of the chord are sustained, but sometimes it is the fifth of the chord that is in motion, ascending in half-steps (and often descending back to the starting place after that) while the other notes of the chord remain in place. A very simple form of CESH is shown in Figure 42 for each of the four possibilities in harmony (in minor with the root in motion, in minor with the fifth in motion; in major with the root in motion; and in major with the fifth in motion). A specific voicing will not be recommended, since it appears in a wide variety of voicings in recorded music, so the voicings in Figure 42 are merely to explain and illustrate the device in simple, clear voicings.

CESH in minor, root in motion.   CESH in major, root in motion.

CESH in minor, 5th in motion.   CESH in major, 5th in motion.

FIGURE 42

The examples shown in Figure 42 can be in half-notes or quarter notes, as well as whole-notes, depending upon the durations of the chords as needed in a particular tune. One of the benefits of encountering a need or opportunity to use CESH is that often 2-4 measures will be consumed while playing a reasonably easy harmonic device (CESH), giving the keyboard player a little time in which to relax or think ahead to something following the CESH that might require more thought.

CESH is a dramatic musical device, one that is likely to tug at the heartstrings, and one which usually appears in songs which have the same intent. It is no coincidence that CESH appears in dramatic ballads like "What Are You Doing For The Rest Of Your Life", "My Funny Valentine", "Round Midnight", "In A Sentimental Mood", "Masquerade", or "Meaning Of The Blues", just to mention a few. Because CESH is a dramatic device, players and singers look for additional opportunities to use it, even in tunes which don't already contain a prescribed CESH, as the device may be used anywhere there is a II-V progression, playing the CESH in the key of the II minor (it overlaps the V as well, as will be shown later). A I chord in minor of long duration is also a target for a CESH.

In chord symbols, CESH might be indicated by one of the following:

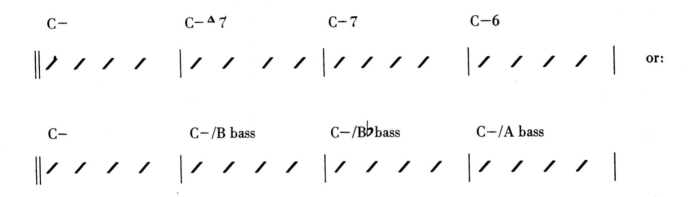

(the chord durations might be two beats, even one beat each, depending upon the particular tune)

If CESH is used in a II-V situation and the bass note is, or the bass player plays the root of the V chord during its assigned duration, then the symbols might appear as:

If CESH were to be played at every II-V situation in a tune like "Lover Man", then it could occur in bars 1-2, 3-4, 9-10, 11-12, 17-18, 21-22, 25-26, and 27-28!

For most of the readership, to merely hear CESH once or twice is sufficient to cause the memory to recall many tunes which use the device. CESH is also very easy to recognize by ear, when it appears on record or in concert. On the following pages is a list of some of the tunes which indicate the use of CESH or tunes on which it has become traditional interpretation to interpolate a CESH segment. Play as many as you can, either from knowing the tune or finding a copy of it somewhere. Look for even more examples.

EXAMPLES OF CESH

(Contrapuntal Elaboration of Static Harmony)

CESH in Minor (root in motion)	Location
After The Loving	3rd bar, 5th bar
Angel Eyes	beginning
A Taste of Honey	beginning
Billy Boy	9th bar
Bittersweet	beginning
Blue Skies	beginning
Bye Bye Blackbird	9th bar
Charade	beginning
Chim Chim Cheree	beginning
Confirmation	bridge (17th bar)
Cry Me A River	beginning
Falling In Love With Love	2nd half of 1st bridge (13th bar)
Feelings	beginning
For Once In My Life	3rd, 5th, and 9th bars
God Bless The Child	bridge (21st measure)
Golden Lady	beginning
I Could Write A Book	2nd bridge (25th bar)
I Feel Like Flying	
In A Sentimental Mood	beginning, 3rd bar
It Don't Mean A Thing	beginning
It Only Takes A Moment	13th bar
Just In Time	bridge (17th bar)
Like Someone In Love	2nd half of 1st bridge (13th bar)
Lover Man	beginning, 3rd bar, and bridge
Masquerade	beginning
Michelle	bridge (13th bar)
More	both bridges (9th, 25th bars)
Music To Watch Girls Go By	beginning
My Favorite Things	beginning
My Funny Valentine	beginning, 9th bar
My Romance	5th bar
Rainy Days and Mondays	
Round Midnight	beginning
Seventh Sign	beginning
Someday My Prince Will Come	5th bar
Strayhorn	3/4 interlude (4 consecutive ex.)
Summertime	beginning
Tenor Madness	9th bar
25 Or 6 To 4	beginning
What Are You Doing For The Rest Of Your Life	beginning

CESH in Minor (5th in motion)	Location
Angel Eyes	beginning
Invitation	beginning
Israel	beginning
James Bond Theme	beginning
Meaning Of The Blues	beginning
Memories Of You	bridge (17th bar)
Old Flame	beginning

CESH in Major (root in motion)	
Bojangles	beginning
Ice Castles	beginning
If	beginning
Truly	beginning
With A Little Help From My Friends	beginning
You Are So Beautiful	beginning

CESH in Major (5th in motion)	
Brazil	beginning
Lucky Southern	introduction
Make Someone Happy	beginning, 5th, 9th bar
Idaho	beginning

There are many ways to voice a CESH other than the simplistic examples used in Figure 42. Some of the possibilities that are in common use are shown in Figure 43 (below). Only minor keys were used in the figure, but only the fourth voicing shown cannot be played in major by simply raising the third of the chord from E♭ to E♮. CESH with the fifth in motion (see the last voicing given in Figure 43) is much less flexible in voicing possibilities, hence only one is shown here. Note that the bass note is sometimes moving alone, other times is doubled in higher voice, and other times it is sustained while an upper voice moves.

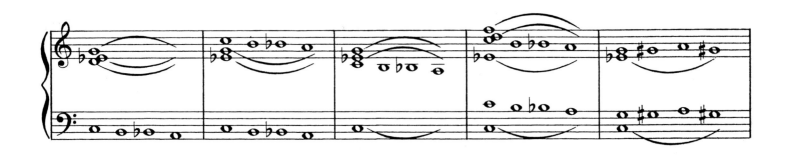

FIGURE 43

These voicings (and others invented by the reader) should be learned well enough to be able to play them in any key.

A distinction should be made between CESH and a number of harmonic devices which are very similar, but different. Some tunes, for example, will have a bass note which is descending, against an unchanging chord, but it descends in whole-steps instead of being chromatic, or it descends a whole-step and then a half-step. Those would be borderline cases of CESH, certainly not the stereotype. Sometimes the tune will have a moving bass note against an unchanging chord, but the motion is diatonic (scale-like), moving down a note sequence like C, B, A, G, C, B, A, G, C, etc. . This is more like a vamping (repetitious) introduction to a brisk, folky or march-like tune, and certainly not CESH. Still other tunes will have a bass line that descends chromatically, but the chord **does** change, like:

C–   G7/B bass   C–/B♭ bass

| /   /   /   / | /   /   /   / | /   /   /   / |

This is not a CESH, either, because by definition ("static harmony") the chord does not change in CESH.

The Dominant Seventh Chord With A Suspended Fourth

This chord is commonly called the **sus. 4** chord, as an abbreviated term. The chord has an interesting history. J.S. Bach used the chord (as did others in his day) two centuries ago, but he always resolved the fourth down a half-step (whole-step on minor chords) to become the third of the chord, in the classic 4-3 suspension or 4-3 appogiatura so closely identified with his musical style (even in parody). Long after Bach's time it became unnecessary to resolve the fourth, becoming the sus. 4 chord, much as the 9-8 suspensions and appogiaturas eventually led to the ninth chord that no longer needed resolving in the mid-nineteenth century. The sus. 4 chord appears in a few old standards, like Strayhorn's "Lush Life" (from the 30's), but it was largely ignored until the 50's. In 1956, Miles Davis recorded "Dear Old Stockholm" to which he added an eight-measure vamping figure between choruses that used a Gm7 with the bassist playing a pedal note of C (this has become one of the ways to describe, define, or symbolize a sus. 4 chord, as a minor seventh chord with a bass note that is a fifth lower than the root of the minor seventh chord). It was rare, incidentally, in those days to sustain any chord for more than four measures, as the recording of "Dear Old Stockholm" predates the invention of modal tunes in jazz. This vamp figure most likely led to Miles' introduction of modal tunes to jazz in the recording of "Milestones", which uses that same chord (Gm7) with a C bass) and even the melody of the "Dear Old Stockholm" vamp in an even more extended way. Ironically, after Miles' next album, **Kind Of Blue**, was assimilated by his many playing admirers, modal tunes focused more on the minor seventh chord (without the pedal note of a fifth lower) as the chord to be elongated for 8-16 bars; i.e., "So What" (from the **Kind Of Blue** album), Coltrane's "Impressions", and Freddie Hubbard's "Mr. Clean". The sus. 4 chord more or less dropped out of sight until Miles' "81" and especially Herbie Hancock's "Maiden Voyage" were released. Suddenly there was an explosion of sus. 4 chords, appearing in tunes by pop artists like Carole King, James Taylor, and Billy Joel, and jazz artists like Hal Galper, Ron Miller, Dan Haerle, Jamey Aebersold, McCoy Tyner, and countless others. In one decade the sus. 4 chord has gone from rarity to become the most popular, significant chord of our time!

Like CESH, the sus. 4 chord is voiced in a variety of ways, with no single voicing predominating. Some of the more common voicings are shown in Figure 44. The first two voicings are for the left hand alone, for those times when the right hand is needed for playing the melody or for an impovised solo. The third voicing is the most common two-handed voicing and the easiest to find. Simply play the root in octaves in the left hand (in a fairly low register) and with the right hand play a major triad (usually in second inversion; that is, spelled as 5-1-3 instead of 1-3-5) whose root is a whole-step lower than the root of the assigned chord. In Figure 44 the voicing is a second inversion B-flat major triad over a C bass. The fourth voicing in the figure is the one used in Herbie Hancock's "Maiden Voyage", though the tune is in a different key. The fifth voicing could be described as a B-flat major seventh chord over a C bass and the sixth one could be thought of as a Gm7(9) chord over C. The seventh voicing in Figure 44 is the favorite of those who prefer a more-clustered spacing. The last voicing is quartal (based on perfect fourth intervals), uses two vertical combinations in the right hand, sounds especially good in modal tunes that use sus. 4 chords in long durations (4-8 bars or more), and is the voicing used by Hal Galper in the recording of his tune, "Reach Out". All the chords in Figure 44 are sus. 4 chords, though some are symbolized differently to suggest an approximate voicing. Those different symbols can also be expected to turn up in fake books and lead sheets once in awhile, as the symbology for the sus. 4 chord is not completely standardized.

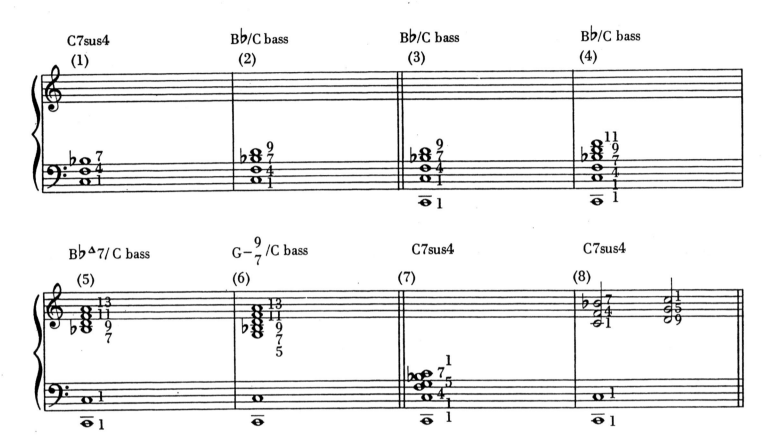

FIGURE 44

Practice the above voicings in different keys and look for other possibilities. You will want to have some alternates, since the chord will appear often. Whole tunes have been written which use only sus. 4 chords, like Hancock's "Maiden Voyage" and Hal Galper's "Spidit" (a sus. 4 blues). Look for such tunes for practicing the sus. 4 voicings.

END OF SECTION 2

SECTION 3

MODAL PLAYING

The "So What" Voicing

Modal tunes are tunes which have extraordinarly long durations on each chord. The durations may be 8-16 measures or even be the **only** chord assigned to the whole tune. We are, then, confronted with a tune-type which doesn't require that we quickly respond to a myriad of chord symbols, but instead requires that we think of interesting ways to enhance and vary just a few chords (if even that many). "So What", from the Miles Davis album. **Kind of Blue**, which was mentioned toward the end of Section 2, used a voicing that was unique in its time, and is commonly refered to as the "So what voicing". It was played by both the keyboard player (Bill Evans) and the horn section (Miles Davis, John Coltrane, and Cannonball Adderly) on that track. One of the most unique aspects of the voicing, shown in Figure 45, was that **two** vertical chord structures were used to realize a single chord, the structures are identical, intervallically, and only a whole-step apart.

FIGURE 45

The above figure was a background to a melody (not shown here) that was played by the bass. Note that both vertical voicings have a major third interval on top and all the other notes are a perfect fourth apart. All of the notes are drawn from a D dorian scale (same as a C major scale that is played from D to D; D, E, F, G, A, B, C, D). A number of interesting aspects surface when the voicing is examined. For starters, by placing the top note of the voicing (B on first one, A on the second) two octaves lower, all the intervals become perfect fourths, as shown in Figure 46.

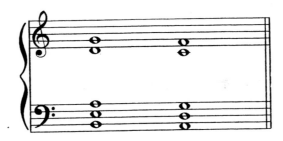

FIGURE 46

Doubtlessly, the creators of the voicing must have realized that this symmetry was possible, but probably rejected it as sounding too academic and lacking the interesting sonority provided by having a major third interval on top.

The next point of interest is the particular placement of the voicings within the D dorian scale. Why place it so that B and A are on top? Why not put D, E, E, F, G, or C on top? Looking at Figure 47, it will be seen that we lose the intervallic structure when one of those notes is on top, except in the case of placing E on top, and a "So What" voicing on E would give us no place with which to alternate (B and A were only a step apart, remember) without encountering an uncomfortable leap or using a voicing that is structured differently than the model. In Figure 47, the brackets indicate those places where either the top interval is only a **minor** third interval, or where the spacing between adjacent lower tones has become an augmented fourth (tri-tone) interval instead of a perfect fourth.

FIGURE 47

Those voicings that are formed on scale degrees where the intervallic structure is not consistent with the model of major third interval on top and perfect fourths below can still be used, and are, but usually as passing sounds rather than sustained voicings.

Another interesting fact that emerges from studying the "So What" voicing is that, when the notes are compressed into a single octave (by changing the octave placement of some of the notes) the result is a **pentatonic scale** (see Figure 48 below).

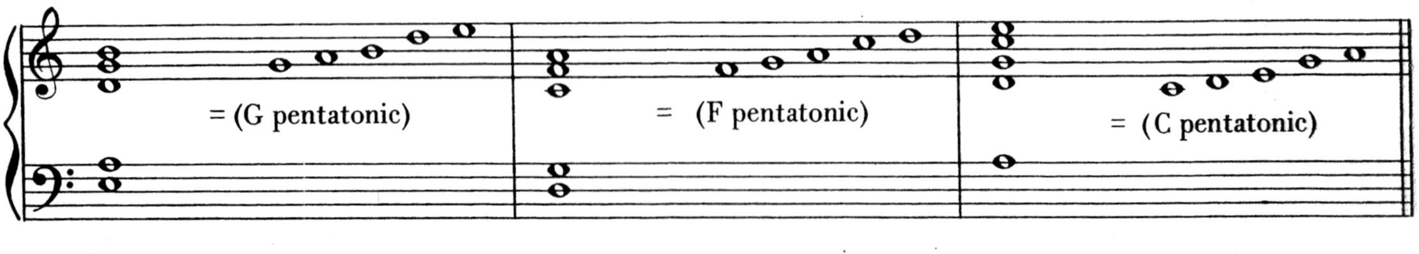

FIGURE 48

Note that the voicing with E on top is included in the above figure, since it is the only other scale degree besides B and A that can be on top and still retain the interval structure that is needed. To the player not acquainted with the craft of improvisation, Figure 48 might not seem so significant, but the serious student of improvisation will note immediately that the G, F, and C pentatonics are precisely the ones that work when improvising on a modal tune that is in D minor (dorian)! We will return to this same phenomenon when we discuss the quartal voicings later in this section.

SIDE—SLIPPING

Since the invention of the "So What" voicing by the Miles Davis group in 1957, its use has expanded considerably. Because modal tunes change chords so seldom, two vertical sounds, even three, for a single chord symbol, will not stem the tide of boredom, and so **side-slipping** was invented. Side-slipping, sometimes called **playing outside**, is a commonly-used device in which an improviser (and usually the keyboard player as well) will deliberately play out-of-key for the sake of adding tension to the line. The device is fully discussed in **The Complete Method For Improvisation**[5]. During a side-slip, the solo line and the keyboard player, using a reasonable amount of melodic or linear symmetry, will often simply modulate at will, most often to a half-step higher, and return to the given key in a rather short time, say 2 to 4 beats in most cases. Like the stretching of a rubber band, the attuned listener seems to know that the player's excursion into another key is very temporary and that he/she will snap back to the original key when the tension period is over. In the meantime, the listener has been taken on a brief trip that has broken the monotony of modality. The point of all this is that the "So What" voicing is often used for this purpose, with the player modulating the voicing at will (in parallel symmetry) to placements belonging to a key very disparate from the given key. Because the voicing is unique and perhaps unfamiliar to the reader, and because the success of a side-slipping venture greatly depends upon the glibness of the execution, it is suggested that the student select the melody to any tune, voice a "So What" voicing under **each** note of the melody, and play it a number of times, just to become adept at side-slipping with ease on the voicing. Understand that the voicings will not sound like the real progression to the tune, nor will it sound like the right key or any single key, but the object here is not to harmonize the melody in some sane fashion, but simply to acquire more flexibility with forming the voicing under any note. The first phrase of a well-known tune is shown in Figure 49 as an illustration of the suggested practice.

FIGURE 49

The "So What" voicing has also been used, by pianists and arrangers, on other chord-types. Look, for example, at Figure 44, voicing No. 2, where the voicing has been suggested as a common realization of the sus. 4 chord. Figure 50 shows the "So What" voicing as it is commonly used on the major seventh chord and the major seventh chord with a raised fourth (+4). By lowering the bottom note one-half step, the voicing can also be used as a dominant seventh chord with a raised fourth, ninth, and thirteenth, as shown in Figure 50.

---

[5] - Ibid, Chapter 2

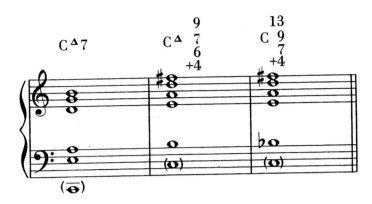

FIGURE 50

Pianists and arrangers sometimes use the "So What" voicing in a parallel fashion, like Figure 49, but in such as way that the first setting of the voicing (and sometimes some of the others) will fit the assigned chord, though others will "go outside" within the melodic phrase, giving the overall illusion of fitting or being consonant (the "outside" settings are then heard as passing chords that are consistent in structure with the "inside" settings). This sort of device usually only lasts for a measure or so, then returns to ordinary voicings (i.e., 1-7-3-5 or rootless voicings and the like). Figure 51 shows an example of this device, used here on the first several measures of the bridge (B section) of Ellington's "In A Sentimental Mood". Figure 52 shows a similar use that was played by Jamey Aebersold on Volume 1 of his play-along series, on the ninth measure of a B-flat blues. Here the device is used in free comping, rather than being aligned with a given melody.

FIGURE 51

FIGURE 52

It is easy to see that, from the uses shown in Figures 49, 51, and 52, the player needs to develop considerable ease with moving the voicing from key to key in order to accomodate parallel and side-slipping needs.

Note that in Figure 52 only four notes appear in each playing of the voicing, instead of five. Because the bottom note is sometimes omitted, it is safer to remember what notes can be on **top** of the voicing, instead of the bottom. In minor seventh chords (dorian) the fifth, sixth, or ninth can be on top. In major seventh chords the major seventh or augmented fourth can be on top, and in sus. 4 chords the ninth is on top.

Quartal Voicings (for the left hand)

When playing modal tunes it is usually more appropriate to space the left hand voicings in fourths, instead of thirds. If all notes are to agree with the dorian scale (most modal tunes are dorian), yet maintain perfect fourth intervals in three-note voicings, five vertical arrangements are possible, as shown in Figure 53, which is in D minor (or D dorian).

FIGURE 53

Although not all intervals are perfect fourths, an additional possibility that is in common use is:

Any or all these voicings, when played with a bassist who is emphasizing the root (D), will express a feeling of D minor, therefore the pianist is free to use as many or as few as he/she wishes. Looking back to Figure 48, it was pointed out that there are three "So What" voicings possible for any dorian minor key, and that each of the three contained the notes of one of the three pentatonic scales possible for dorian minor. Now looking at Figure 53, we see that if only the top notes of the five quartal voicings are read, they spell an F pentatonic scale, if only the middle notes are read, they spell a C pentatonic scale, and if only the bottom notes are read, they spell a G pentatonic scale. This is not only interesting to note, but it also gives us a quick system for finding the five quartal voicings in any dorian minor key. Simply place the third of the dorian key on top, space the hand in perfect fourths, and move them (parallel) up the intervals of a pentatonic scale (1,2,3,5,6)! In essence, this is akin to playing all three of the possible pentatonic sclaes simultaneously.

When executing a side-slipping phrase with the left hand quartel voicings it will obviously be a strain to quickly find all five of the quartal voicings in a new, temporary, unrelated key (i.e., a half-step higher). To solve this problem understand that most pianists will only use two or three of the possible five, and since the side-slip sounds best if it is consistent, even symmetrical, with the preceding 'inside' phrase, we're really only having to come up with, say, two voicings in the new key. Consequently, pianists will often use something like what is shown in Figure 54, which is not very difficult.

FIGURE 54

Figure 54 illustrates only a couple of countless possibilities, but by practicing these examples and inventing others for practice, it is easy to see that the goal of using a couple of quartal voicings in a side-slip poses no great problem.

While the left hand is playing quartal voicings in a modal tune, the right hand can improvise upon the dorian scale or any of all of the three pentatonic scales for that particular key. When one hand side-slips, the other hand should, also, in most cases. It is awkward, at first, to attempt a side-slip, but by adding a right hand improvisation to a pattern like the one shown in Figure 54, repeating the pattern over and over, it eventually becomes quite easy and natural to do so.

Contemporary Chord Symbols

Classical music and rock music frequently make use of inverted chords; that is, chords in which the third, fifth, or seventh of the chord is on the bottom instead of the root (even the bassist is assigned to play one of those notes, contrary to our rootless voicings in which the bassist will probably play the root of the chord). This practice has seldom occured in jazz, traditionally. It is, however, becoming increasingly common in modern jazz, sometimes in very complex ways. The chord symbol in such cases will usually involve a relatively simple, traditional chord symbol, but with a different bass note, similar to the ones shown in Figure 44 in No. 2-6, using a slanted line (╱) between the chord symbol and the assigned bass note. Sometimes the word "bass" (see Figure 44) does not show, because whatever pitch name follows the slanted line is understood (by common practice) to be the bass note. Sometimes the bass note is a member of the chord (like we find in classical and rock music), sometimes it is merely a member of the chord-**scale**, and other times the bass note is totally foreign to the chord or chord-scale. Figure 55 shows some of the various possibilities one might expect to encounter, along with an **example** of how it **might** be voiced. In voicing symbols of this sort, the bass note often sounds best played in octaves, in a low register, with the right hand (usually alone) playing the chord symbol that appears on the left of the slanted line, in a register somewhat removed form the bass note.

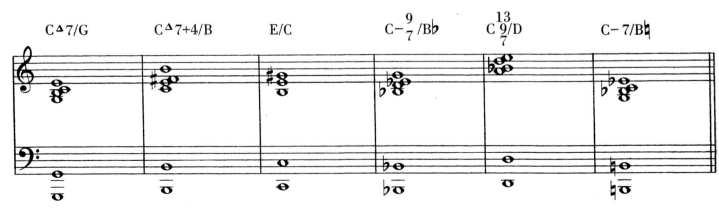

FIGURE 55

Although some of the examples in Figure 55, especially the last one, may sound unlikely, even absurd, to the reader, **all** of them come from actual music encountered by the author, and each sounds very effective when played in context with the piece from which it derives. Although many new ones are likely to be invented, their interpretation is likely to be similar to what is shown in Figure 55 and therefore should present no problem to the reader.

Another type of chord symbol is the **polychord** (playing of more than one chord simultaneously). Its symbol is similar to the ones which appear in Figure 55, but quite different. Two lettered symbols appear again, but this time they are separated by a **horizontal** line and **both** symbols are **chord** symbols, rather than one of them being merely a bass note. Often a polychordal symbol is simply a different way of showing an added to (ninths, elevenths, thirteenths) or altered chord, and giving it a distinctive organizational sound by having the two chords be sounded in their own registers. Page 68 of **Improvising Jazz 6** shows a chart of all polychordal possibilities. Figure 56 shows a sampling of those possibilities.

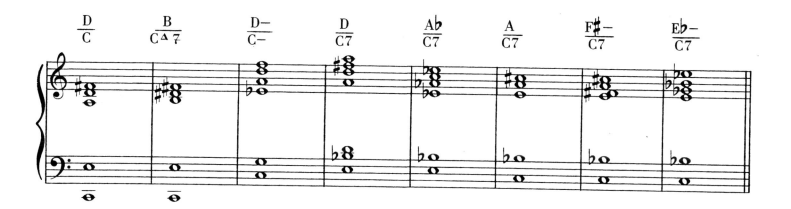

FIGURE 56

Idiomatic Keyboard Vamps

Sometimes a pianist is confronted with the need to provide more than the realization of a given set of chord symbols to a specific tune, owing to the fact that the tune may carry with it a specific, vamp-like interpretation with specific voicings and rhythms, without which the tune simply doesn't resemble its recorded model. A tune like "Maiden Voyage" by Herbie Hancock, with its very sparse melody, is recognized by most players and audiences because of the characteristic vamp that accompanies the melody, not the melody itself. Because of this, a pianist not familiar with the tune might make the mistake of reading the chord symbols only to discover that the other players in the group and the audience are hardly able to recognize the tune without its familiar (to them) keyboard vamp. There are a number of tunes that fall into this category, some of which are shown on the following pages. The conscientious student will feel compelled to learn and memorize these vamps and others like them.

6 - Coker, Prentice-Hall, Englewood Cliffs, N.J., 1964

IDIOMATIC KEYBOARD VAMPS

Watermelon Man (Herbie Hancock)

Cantaloupe Island (Herbie Hancock)

All Blues (Miles Davis)

Killer Joe (Benny Golson)

Coral Keys (Cedar Walton)

What Was (Chick Corea)

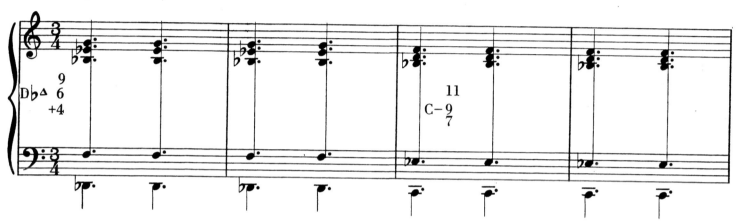

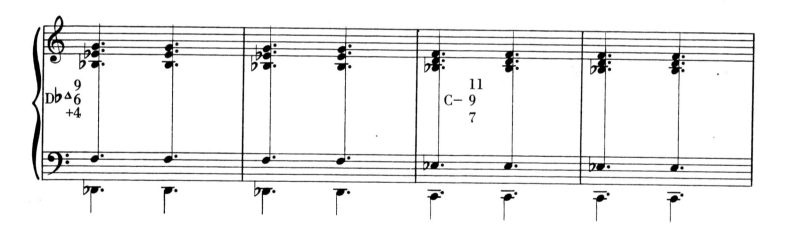

So What (Miles Davis)

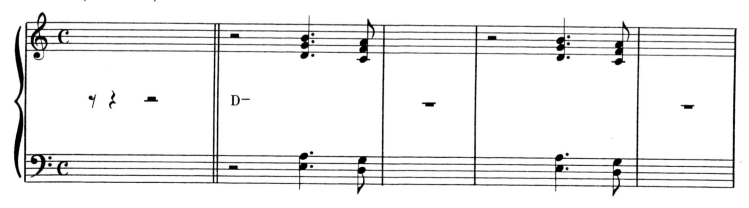

Mahjong (Wayne Shorter)

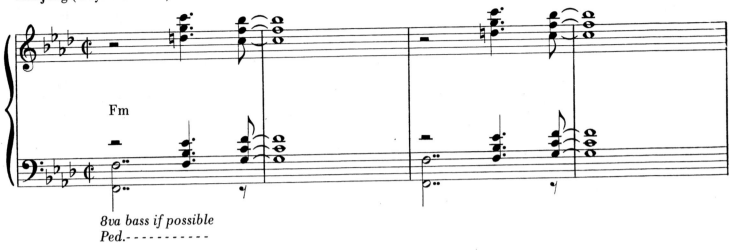

Fm

8va bass if possible
Ped.- - - - - - - - - - -

Maiden Voyage (Herbie Hancock)

Dsus4$\frac{9}{7}$

Fsus4$\frac{9}{7}$

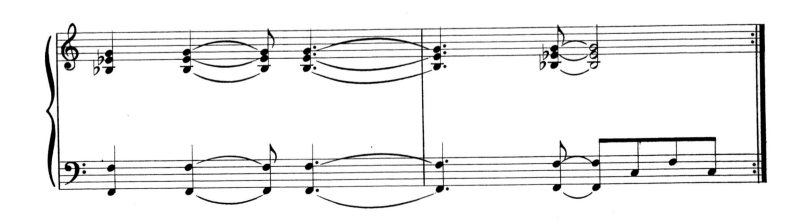

The idiomatic keyboard vamps shown on the preceding pages do not show the melody, nor is a complete chorus of the vamp given. Because of the latter, the player needs to learn to adapt the vamps shown here to the remainder of the progression, in most cases. For example, the second chord of "Cantaloupe Island" is a D-flat seventh chord, so the character of the F minor vamp shown may be contined thusly:

Transcribed Solos

Although it is not the purpose of this book to explain or teach improvisation, the importance of playing transcribed solos should at least be mentioned. It would be possible, after all, to learn all that has been presented here (voicings, progressions, symbols, exercises, CESH, idiomatic keyboard vamps, etc.) and still be confronted with a naive-sounding right hand, when soloing. Prolonged listening to great jazz pianists on record (and live, whenever possible) cannot be over-emphasized here. When a person impovises, he/she draws from everything that has been heard or played in prior experiences. It is important, therefore, to fill the ears and memory with the best sounds the music has to offer. Playing transcriptions of great solos (many, many times!) ingrains each individual phrase, so that they may come to the mind and hands during an improvisation, though perhaps in a slightly permutated, individualized manner of expression. Many piano solos have been transcribed and published on the open market, some appear in illegal publications, and still others could be transcribed by the reader.

END OF SECTION 3

APPENDIX
(Teacher's Supplement)

Who Should Teach Jazz Keyboard?

If the course is to be taken by non-pianists (that is, musicians whose primary instrument is something other than piano), it is a good idea to have a teacher who is also a non-pianist, but one who has learned to use the piano, perhaps as an arranger, a teacher of improvisation, or as a strong secondary instrument (especially one who has played piano on professional engagements), or possibly one who has successfully completed a jazz keyboard course similar to the one presented here. This is not to say that a pianist would not be a good teacher for jazz keyboard, but if the course is to be open to non-pianists, the students may be more intimidated by a pianist, they may surmise that the pianist/teacher can't possibly understand their problems with trying to play piano, or they may simply not believe that their potential is as promising as that of the teacher. A traditionally-trained pianist may indeed have problems, too, such as not being acclimated to the jazz style, not knowing enough tunes, or spending too much time with keyboard calisthenics (posture, finger technique, touch, scale fingerings, reading, etc.). All these things are important, to be sure, especially to the student pianist, but the first task is to overcome a lack of confidence, in most cases, and to produce immediate, practical results. If the pianist/teacher can control these obstacles, then they may be a better choice even than a non-pianist/teacher.

The teacher needs to have a well-developed set of musical ears, unless he/she plans to spend each class hour in constant motion, walking around the room continously to be sure that each student is performing the tasks accurately by watching their every move, instead of knowing by hearing. Simply saying that what a student has played is "wrong" is not enough, either. The teacher needs to be able to recognize the exact nature of the problem and solve it quickly, with statements like "E-flat", your right hand has slipped one step too high", "minor seventh, not dominant", or "lower the top note by a half-step".

The teacher should know a good number of tunes, as they may need to be called into play at any moment for purposes of illustration or demonstration.

Enrollment Considerations

It has been the experience of this author that many students are interested in a course like the one presented in this book. Here at the University of Tennessee, with a music department that only services 100-150 music majors, Jazz Piano I has drawn 15-20 students every time around, which is three times each school year (45-60 students annually), in spite of the fact that it has been in operation for eight years! Ideally, the class size should be more like 10-15, depending upon the number of pianos in the keyboard room. One or two weekly meetings is sufficient to the task and allows preparation time between classes. Expect fewer students for the second level and still fewer for the third level, hence the offering at Tennessee (which is on a quarter system, that is, three terms between September and June) is organized thusly:

Fall Quarter . . . . Jazz Piano I and II (2 separate classes)
Winter Quarter. . . . . Jazz Piano I and II
Spring Quarter . . . . Jazz Piano I and III

In this way level I is offered three times a year, level II twice a year, and level III once a year.

Expect a disparity of levels, backgrounds, and abilities. Don't be discouraged by this, as students learn from each other. Also, no one feels out-of-place when the range is so wide and complex, though they might if all other members of the class were exactly alike. Don't be surprised if non-pianists do better in the course than the pianists. Knowing the piano is one thing, but the <u>desire</u> to learn the content of the course, even the <u>ability</u> to learn the content is quite another. Though the reasons are not exactly clear, this author often <u>finds</u> that the best students in the class are <u>most</u> often <u>percussionists</u> (despite the derision they are often forced to endure as music students)!

<u>Course Materials</u>

Obviously the course will be more efficiently realized if each student has a copy of the text, as it will alleviate the need for the teacher to explain and illustrate each and every item taken up. Furthermore, the members of the class will understand new theories and learn new techniques at a varying rates of speed, so that the slow learner can re-read passages in the text as many times as needed, instead of being at the mercy of the brief explanation that might take place in class, and the faster students can work at their own pace and learn to perform some of the more thorough-going suggestions contained in the method.

The teacher should plan to include additional tune progressions, hopefully with melodies and titles, to round out the class' experience. Fake books, published songbooks, Aebersold books like Volumes 22, 23, and 25 (which can be purchased separately from the play-along records), and self-prepared tunes in a hand-out form are possibilities for inclusion. <u>Improvising Jazz</u> has 83 commonly-played tune progressions in Roman Numerals, given in Appendix D. A new publication by Mike Tracy called <u>Pocket Changes</u> contains the chord progressions to 335 commonly-played jazz tunes, and is available for $6.75 by writing to Pocket Changes, P.O. Box 86, Jeffersonville, Indiana, 47130. This book is an excellent collection of tunes; accurate, and convenient.

Play-along records and tapes are very helpful to use in class, in that they closely approximate a realistic playing situation with bass and drums, help maintain tempos, and, when the piano channel is left on, provide insight and inspiration when needed. Aebersold's Volumes 1 and 3 are especially helpful when exercising II-V's and II-V-I's. Volume 2 (<u>Nothin' But Blues</u>) is a great digest on the blues. Volume 5 has a good track for practicing modal playing, called "Snap, Crackle, and Pop." Volumes 16 and 21 have good exercise tracks, like Volumes 1 and 3, and of course the 42 standard tunes contained in Volumes 22, 23, and 25 are most helpful. The accompaniment tape for <u>The Complete Method For Improvisation</u> (Coker) contains a track called "Interminable" that works well for practicing modal playing.

Experience has shown this teacher that it is important to give students a proficiency syllabus at the beginning of the course, so that they know what they are responsible for, and approximately when. It also permits them to work at their own pace. The following page is a sample proficiency sheet for level I. The individual instructor should design his/her own version to suit individual tastes and needs. The number of items can be increased or decreased and adjustments made to allow for a 16, 20, or 32-meeting course or for a 1 or 2-term course instead of 3.

On the page following the Proficiency Syllabus is another sample page, this one showing a simple way for the instructor to keep records on the progress of each student. To save space, some of the items are coded or abbreviated, such as <u>P S-W</u> (parallel "So What" voicings) and <u>IKV</u> (Idiomatic Keyboard Vamps). The items on the far right (after the double line) are components of the final exam, <u>S/R</u> standing for sight-reading (of chord symbols), <u>P.P.</u> meaning prepared piece, and <u>M</u> standing for modal playing.

PROFICIENCY SYLLABUS

Music 2810
Jazz Piano I

This class meets one day (Monday) per week at 1:15. There will be, then, about 10 class meetings. Listed below are a series of skills which must be ably demonstrated by each student in a brief examination at the beginning of any class he/she chooses. Most students should elect to attempt only one of the 5 items (listed below) at a time. Grading of these items will be PASS/FAIL only, and once the student has passed an item he/she is free to move on to the next skill to be acquired. Most students should also choose to take their exams shortly after (1-2 weeks) the item has been introduced in class. NO STUDENT WILL BE PERMITTED TO TAKE A FINAL EXAM (which is graded A-F) WHO HAS NOT COMPLETED SUCCESSFULLY ALL 5 ITEMS. In such cases, the student will receive an "I" if he/she has completed 3 or more items, and an automatic "F" for fewer than 3 items. It is sincerely felt that all 5 skills can be easily accomplished in 10 weeks of no more than 1 hour of daily practice. It is also believed that any student who can successfully perform these skills will be assured an easy time with the final examination... and probably a high grade.

SKILL TO BE ACQUIRED	SUGGESTED (APPROXIMATE) TIME FOR EXAMINATION
1-7-3-5 voicing, diatonically, in the keys (major) of G, B-flat, and D-flat.	Class Meeting 2 or 3
1-7-3-5 voicing, in II-7, V7 progression (using 1-3-7-9 on V7), in 12 keys.	Class Meeting 3 or 4
1-7-3-5 voicing, II-V-I (in major) progression, in 12 keys, using 9ths on the II and I chords, 9ths and 13ths on the V chords.	Class Meeting 5 or 6
1-7-3-5 voicing, IIϕ7, V7 (with an altered 9th) I— progression, in 12 keys.	Class Meeting 7 or 8
Blues voicings (7-3-13 and 3-7-9, left hand only), blues progression (memorized), and right hand improvisation on blues scales.	Class Meeting 8 or 9

ORDER IN WHICH TUNES WILL BE TAKEN UP (from Aebersold, Volume 25)
(1) The Party's Over (slow)
(2) Summertime (medium)
(3) Have You Met Miss Jones (fast)
(4) I Could Write A Book (fast)
(5) I've Grown Accustomed (slow)
(6) I Can't Get Started (slow)
(7) September Song (medium)
(8) It Might As Well Be Spring (slow)
(9) Come Rain or Shine (medium)
(10) A Foggy Day (fast)
(11) Love Is Here To Stay (fast)

JAZZ PIANO I	1-7-3-5 diatonically G, B♭, D♭	1-7-3-5 II-V 12 Keys	1-7-3-5-9 II-V-I 12 Keys	1-7-3-5 II°7 V7 ♭9 I- 12 Keys	BLUES VOICINGS 2 inversions C, F, B♭, E♭, G	PREP. PIECE	BLUES	S/R

JAZZ PIANO II	3-5-7-9 II-V-I 12 Keys	7-9-3-5+ II-V-I Mdm 12 Keys	CESH	sus. 4	PS-W	MODAL VOICINGS	IKV	P.P.	IKV	M	S/R
	1-7-3-5 diatonically G, B♭, D♭	1-7-3-5 II-V	1-7-3-5-9 II-V-I	1-7-3-5 II°7 V7 ♭9 I-	BLUES VOICINGS 2 inversions C, F, B♭, E♭, G						

Checkpoints For Assisting Students

The following points are arranged in chronological order, as they would arise while using Jazz Keyboard as a text. They are not necessarily all the points that should be mentioned, but the ones which through personal experience seem to be the most consistently helpful to the class.

(1) after the students have played the diatonic seventh chord exercises shown in Exercise 1, in C, E-flat, G, B-flat, and D-flat, ask them to produce isolated chords from those keys, using the list shown on page 14;

(2) make the students aware of the inevitable ear-training made possible by their study. Play the II-V and II-V-I progression for them, in any key, even changing the voicing, and ask them what you've played, so they become aware and confident about recognizing the sound of the progression. When a student self-corrects a voicing for the obvious reason that it didn't sound right, remind him/her that it was an improving ear that recognized the error. When the students play their II-V- and II-V-I progressions in various modulation sequences (by choice), ask the others in the class what that modulation sequence was (i.e., down in half-steps, up in half-steps, down in whole-steps, around the cycle, etc.) and ask the others whether or not ninths and thirteenths were added;

(3) when the tune progressions are beginning to be read, help the class to learn to recognize the lettered II-V and II-V-I progressions by asking them to look for 2 or 3 successive letters from the cycle of fifths and look for sequences of the proper chord-types (minor sevenths, dominant sevenths, and major sevenths, in that order). Suggest to them that they bracket those segments for a while.

(4) don't forget to use the montuno exercise for II-V's, as suggested on page 18.

(5) as the class reads the progression to a tune, play the melody for them, so they begin to build the association between melody and chords. At other times play walking bass lines while they're comping the chords. At still other times improvise while they're chording;

(6) when the rootless blues voicings have been introduced, demonstrate the tri-tone phenomenon discussed on page 31 by playing only the bottom two notes of the blues voicings while improvising with the right hand, first in G, then in D-flat;

(7) help the students to select the best inversions for the blues, depending upon the key (sometimes it doesn't make any difference, but sometimes, because of range considerations it does matter);

(8) at the beginning of Section 2, urge the students to learn the two inversions for the II-V-I progression (rootless voicings) as soon as possible (by working a little harder), as there is the danger, at this point, that they may get discouraged before the voicings can be put to work in playing tunes. Once they are under way with playing tunes, their enjoyment will increase and they'll be out of danger;

(9) help the students to determine which inversion is best for a given tune, and when, within a given tune, it might be necessary to change inversions;

(10) when taking up the study of CESH, urge the students to come up with additional tune examples. Though the given list is quite long, there are others, and new ones are invented every day;

(11) when the sus. 4 chord has been presented, ask individuals, at the next meeting, to produce the chord in the various keys called out by you, quickly, in the manner of an aural quiz. Teach them the progressions to tunes which use the sus. 4 chord exclusively, like Herbie Hancock's "Maiden Voyage", Hal Galper's "Spidit", and Jamey Aebersold's "One Step Sideways";

(12) when the "So What" voicing has been taken up, have each student select a tune of his/her choice and voice each note of the melody in that voicing, as a prepared assignment, like the examples shown in Figures 49 and 51.

JERRY COKER is an educator of wide experience, having developed studio music and jazz programs for Indiana University, Sam Houston State University, and the University of Miami. He has been an instructor at the National Stage Band Camps, the Tanglewood Camp (New England Conservatory), and, for the past three summers, the Jerry Coker Summer Camps. In addition, he is well-known for his involvement with the Combo Improvisation Clinics directed by Jamey Aebersold.

Mr. Coker is also recognized as an outstanding performing musician and has been featured as a soloist with Stan Kenton, Woody Herman, Clare Fischer, and Frank Sinatra. In 1970 he was a soloist with the Boston Symphony Orchestra in a jazz piece by Gunther Schuller.

Currently on the faculty of the University of Tennessee at Knoxville, Mr. Coker is concentrating on the development of the new Studio Music and Jazz Program. Course offerings include Improvisation, Arranging, Jazz Pedagogy, Jazz Keyboard, Jazz History, and training for performance in both large and small ensembles.

A prolific author, Mr. Coker has written a number of books on jazz study, which have become standard definitive texts the world over.